Between the Lines

The Mental Skills of Hitting for Softball

Yasmin Mossadeghi, M.S.
and Patti Laguna, Ph.D.

Wish Publishing
Terre Haute, Indiana
www.wishpublishing.com

LCCN: 2006933456

Printed in the United States of America
10 9 8 7 6 5 4 3 2 1

Editorial assistance provided by Dorothy Chambers
Cover designed by Phil Velikan
Cover photo by Jupiter Images
Softball figures at the chapter opening pages used by agreement with www.clipart.com. Cartoons used with the permission of Universal Press Syndicate
Interior photos by Yasmin Mossadeghi and Matt Brown Photography.

Published by
Wish Publishing
P.O. Box 10337
Terre Haute, IN 47801, USA
www.wishpublishing.com

Distributed in the United States by
Cardinal Publishers Group
222 Hillside Avenue, Suite 100
Indianapolis, IN 46218
www.cardinalpub.com

To my family and friends for their constant love and depend-ability. Also, to Ken Ravizza for showing me that mental skills are not just a set of tools used for a particular activity, but a way of living your life.

— Yasmin

To Mom and Dad for all their never-ending support, both dur-ing my softball days (playing and coaching) and all my educa-tional endeavors.

— Patti

Acknowledgments

Special thanks to Patti Laguna for the hard work and dedication she put into this book. To my coaches Judi Garman, Michelle Gromacki and Kelly Ford for making a huge positive impact in my life by inspiring me to be a softball coach. And thanks to all CSUF softball alumni, playersorganization and university (Deb Hartwig always tells me, "Once a TITAN always a TITAN!").

Thank you to the following people for their important and special contributions: Ken Ravizza, Connie Clark, Amber Hall, Tmara Poppe, Mary Jo Firnbach, Cassie Morales, Tanya Rose, Glenn Moore, Kelly Levesque, Kirk Walker, Kelly Peterson, Adrienne Also, Kate Drohan, Carri Leto, Erin Mobley, Sue Enquist, the two UCLA softball players I interviewed, Scott Centala, Aimee Minor, Kristen Rivera, Kim Ogee, Jenny Topping, Kellyn Tate, "my manager and consultant" Jamie Birk, Matt Brown, Universal Press and Wish Publishing.

Last but not least to the sport of softball: If it were not for the game I have grown to love and respect, I would not be here today experiencing and appreciating life with all the people I have met along the way. Softball has been an important part of my past and will continue to be an integral part of my future.

— Yasmin

Special thanks to Yasmin for all the hard work and persistence she put into this book. Thank you to all the softball players who agreed to have their brains picked. And thank you to Holly Kondras and Wish Publishing for recognizing the value of the mental side of performance.

— Patti

Table of Contents

Introduction

What you put in is what you get out

Many people pick up a book because it looks interesting. What they get from a book depends on whether they read the whole book, fully understand it, and absorb and apply the content. As far as reading this book, if you want to understand the concepts being explained regarding the mental game of hitting, you should read this book from beginning to end. Early chapters explain mental skills and steps to improve your performance. As the chapters progress, some skills are repeated but not explained in depth a second time. We recommend reading this book from the first chapter to the end, and if needed, going back to specific chapters throughout the season to refresh your memory on the areas you are having trouble with. If you are like most people, you probably forget the stuff you have read and need to review later. This book was written so that the softball player could refer to it whenever she needed help with the mental game of hitting.

If you read this book like most students read a book (rush through it, skipping chapters), don't expect to get an

"That's my mom. Quick, do what **I** always do: Mentally tune her out."

A in hitting. The individuals who get A's read the books until they fully understand the concepts the author is trying to get across. It's your choice and something you can control: you will get out of this book as much as you put into it.

Everyone is different

In the sport of softball, there are many different ways to excel at hitting. Some excel by hitting home runs, slapping, bunting, being confident or being mentally tough. Whatever the case may be, every hitter prepares in a different way to achieve her own success. One elite hitter may often use the mental game with her hitting, and another may never use the mental game at all. As you read through this book, you will find that many of the top collegiate and national players may describe their thoughts and approach to hitting differently, but they're all top-level hitters in constant pursuit of being the best.

How the mental game works

The mental game of softball is a very complex subject. There are many factors such as anxiety and distraction that can cloud a player's hitting performance. Many young softball players don't understand the mental game, partly because coaches and parents don't understand it, and partly because there are so many other sports and activities in which young players are involved. Players who do understand the mental game at an early age are typically involved in only one sport and have someone (such as a coach, parent or friend) introducing them to the mental skills.

When athletes decide to take softball seriously, the sport becomes a full-time job, and rarely do they have time to play other sports or participate in other activities. The pressures of performing well on a team and practicing year round help athletes meet not only the physical demands of the sport but the mental demands as well. The player soon realizes what it means to be nervous going up to bat, to let other people distract her, and to feel not in control of a situation. This is where the mental game comes into play. Mental skills such as goal setting, self-talk, pre-performance routines and imagery can help the hitter's performance. Play-

> In high school my coach had us do a lot of visualization. We would watch videos of different pitchers to see how they threw and to visualize hitting different pitches in preparation for our games.
>
> *- Kelly Peterson,*
> *Oregon State*
> *University*

ers use these strategies to reduce the anxiety they feel in pressure situations, to help them to know what they can and can't control in situations, and to help block distractions that may disturb them at bat.

Both elite players and non-elite players use mental skills whether they know it or not. For example, when a player says, "I'm just going to stop thinking and hit the ball," it is part of the mental game. Everything a player decides to do becomes part of a "plan" which is the mental game. It is probably a poor way to approach an at-bat but the player is exercising mental skills. There is no switch to turn mental skills on and off; they exist everywhere and with everything we do.

Players admit they use mental skills in their everyday life, in school, at the work place, and at home. If they're in a stressful situation, they use breathing or imagery to calm themselves down. The benefits of using mental skills go far beyond the game of softball; they are a way of life. If players enjoy using mental skills for hitting, they will find that

> My dad and my brother introduced me to mental skills when I was in 12-and-under softball, but I never really bought into it until college. I figured out that being simple and just seeing the ball and hitting it was a plan. Having a plan was a part of the mental game, it doesn't have to involve thinking so much. That's when it started making sense to me.
>
> *-Kim Ogee,*
> *Sacramento Sunbirds*
> *(University of Nebraska)*

they will use them in other areas of their lives as well.

Confidence

Confidence is the biggest reason that hitters are good. If you have confidence in yourself and believe you can get the job done, most likely you will do exactly what you set out to do. If you have only 50 percent confidence in yourself, you will probably execute successfully about 50 percent of the time. When asked if they are confident in themselves, many softball players will say yes, but deep down inside there is a little doubt. That little doubt can spread like a disease and kill off confidence. You must fully believe and convince yourself that you can handle any situation and are one of the best. This doesn't mean you should be cocky, but there should be no hesitation when asked to perform certain executions (e.g., a squeeze, slap and run, etc.).

Having confidence doesn't happen easily. You'll find that you will experience much insecurity as a player as well as many emotional battles as to how good of a player you think you are. People's opinions and statistics can be your enemy when trying to be confident. But when it comes down to it, you'll realize that *you* will probably be your own worst critic. It may take months and even years before you develop the type of confidence that enhances performances. You'll find many players perform their best during their senior year (in high school or college) because their confidence is at its highest. Fear is not an option anymore. These players take on a "now or never" attitude and don't want any regrets when their playing days are done.

Success

You will find that when you read through this book "success" is mentioned quite often. There is no one definition for success because it is something each hitter must define for herself. It can be anything from having the game-winning hit to putting a bunt down to advance the runner. Being a part of a Division I softball program or a top 25 team, or getting a scholarship can also indicate success. However you choose to define success, it should be something that makes you feel good. As you go through this book, you will need to define what success means to you and how you hope to achieve it for your softball hitting.

Chapter 1
Mental Skills

Elite softball players utilize mental skills to increase their performance consistency and ability. Using mental skills enables a hitter to incorporate a variety of problem-solving methods to consistently raise their level of performance and help them reach their potential. The mental game is used by softball players from young to old. In a softball game, mental skills can be used for pregame preparedness all the way to postgame evaluations. Some of the commonly used mental skills include imagery, goal setting, self-talk and pre-performance routines. The goal of using these mental skills is to help athletes consistently reach peak levels of performance by eliminating or decreasing incorrect mental or physical emotional responses, which then allows the maximum transfer of learning from practice settings to the competitive setting (Suinn, 1980).

Softball hitters usually spend hours and hours learning to hit the ball. But hitting a softball consistently and effectively takes more than mere technical practice. It takes mental practice as well. Mental practice involves what you

are thinking about before, during and after each swing. Hitting in softball is a game of failure. When you think about
it, the best hitters fail seven out of 10 at-bats (Joseph, 2002).
So the idea is to rethink the hitting situation from failing
seven out of 10 at-bats to having "quality" at-bats. A quality at-bat is a successful execution of what has been called
by the coach. For example, a quality at-bat in a bunt situation means the hitter executes the bunt. While the hitter
typically gets thrown out at first base, the runner(s) will
advance. Emphasis needs to be directed away from the statistics recorded in the scorebook, such as the batting average, and toward the successful execution of each at-bat.
Therefore to enhance hitting performance the hitter needs
to control her thinking and have a set plan in mind before

stepping into the batter's box. She needs to know exactly what she is trying to accomplish with each at-bat.

Imagery

Imagery involves using all five senses — hearing, smelling, seeing, tasting, and touching — to create or recreate a past, present or future experience in the mind (Vealey, 1986). In other words, it is a process in which the person formulates a movie or scene in her mind, similar to daydreaming. Images can be from an internal or external perspective and can be positive or negative.

Types of imagery

1) Internal imagery occurs when an athlete views the images as though she were inside her body, experiencing all the sensations which might be expected in the actual situation (Cumming & Ste-Marie, 2001). In other words, it is the view the athlete sees through her own eyes, and her feel of the particular movement being executed. For example, a hitter can relive any at-bat using internal imagery to re-experience seeing the pitcher, feeling the swing, and hearing the fans chanting and cheering in the stands.

2) External imagery occurs when the athlete views herself as if she were watching herself in the movies or on videotape (Weinberg & Gould, 1999). A softball hitter can use external imagery to create or re-create a moment when she sees herself hitting a home run

from the viewpoint of the stands or the dugout. Batters can use both kinds of imagery interchangeably depending on the situation and the purpose of the image. If imagery is used correctly, a hitter can imagine any situation that may occur and rehearse the options that can be executed in that situation.

3) Positive imagery occurs when the hitter visualizes a successful at-bat execution such as hitting a home run or putting down a bunt.

4) Negative imagery occurs when an athlete visualizes an unsuccessful execution such as striking out or popping up.

A hitter can use imagery in many ways. Images can be used to recall past experiences and to create or problem-solve new situations. A hitter can recall a home run they hit a couple games ago or a game-winning hit. It is important that softball players use imagery to recall past situations in order to replicate that success (positive imagery) or to figure out what went wrong (negative imagery). Positive imagery is important in maximizing the hitter's potential because it will allow the batter to increase her confidence. It's like watching a batting highlight tape on television with all her greatest hitting experiences. When the batter is hitting in her image, she sees the ball more clearly than ever before, takes perfect swings and hits every ball perfectly (Cluck, 2002). Negative imagery can also be used to enhance performance. Rather than dwelling on the fact that she struck out or popped up, a hitter recalls exactly what went wrong and then imagines herself correcting the problem.

In addition to recalling a past experience, a hitter can create an image of a specific situation she has not yet experienced. This created image allows the hitter to run through a variety of problem-solving options in that particular situation. For example, the hitter imagines herself at the bottom of the seventh inning with a 2-2 count and one out. The winning run is on third base, and a third base bunt signal has been given by the coach. The hitter can imagine squaring around, seeing an inside fastball, and catching the ball with the bat pointed toward the third baseline. The hitter can imagine the same image with a curve ball, with a rise, with a drop, etc. She can rehearse situations she has never experienced before.

> When I'm lying in bed I will go through my hitting stance at least 100 times. I can do it to where it's almost real. I step in the box, imagine the pitcher pitching different pitches and envision myself hitting the ball.
>
> *- Tamara Poppe,*
> *University of Texas*

Application

Imagery can used anywhere and at any time. Here are some specific instances where you might use imagery:

- After an at-bat (remember what pitches were thrown to you and analyze what adjustments you need to make for your next at-bat).

- Before an at-bat (imagine what the pitcher might pitch and how you are going to hit the ball).

- Off a tee or front toss (imagine what pitcher you will be facing and make it seem like a pitcher is pitching to you).

- At home in bed (recall a recent game or times when you were hitting well, or recall unsuccessful performances and what you would do differently to change the outcome).

When preparing for performance make sure to engage in positive images — see yourself getting a hit or a home run, or executing a bunt successfully. You want to imagine positively because it increases the probability of performing well in real life. You should never visualize yourself doing badly, such as striking out or popping up, prior to performance. It will only make it harder to see yourself performing well. Negative imagery and problem-solving imagery should be used only after performance to analyze what went wrong.

Lastly, practice your imagery. Start with simple images and move on to more complex ones. If you find that you have a hard time visualizing, then practice basic exercises like visualizing what your bat looks like, picking up your bat, feeling the bat in your hands, etc. Once these simpler images are easy to see, add more to the image, such as walking into the on-deck circle, stepping into the batter's box, or making the perfect swing and hitting a home run. The more you practice your imagery, the faster and easier it will be to recall yourself hitting when you need to feel good or remember what happened during your last at-bat.

Goal setting

One of the best and most widely used techniques to improve performance for an athlete is goal setting. Goal setting is the act of setting goals to reach a specific objective. An athlete's goal must be reachable, yet challenging enough to take her skills to a higher level. For example, a softball player may have her goal of getting a hit every game, but something more specific such as having a quality at-bat while working on her pre-performance routine will challenge and enhance the player's skill level in the long run. Such a goal also helps to keep the hitter's mind off the outcome of the at-bat while hitting. All hitters have experienced a good solid hit where the defense makes an outstanding play that results in an out. In the scorebook that at-bat is recorded as an out. But that hitter shouldn't be looking to make swing changes, because it was the defensive play that determined the outcome of the at-bat, not the hitting performance. On the other hand, all hitters have experienced a poorly hit ball that results in a hit or a run. The poor hit should be analyzed and changes should be made to swing technique or hitting strategy to allow for better contact.

Short/Long-term goals

The approach to goal setting is different among athletes. There are short-term goals that can be accomplished in a short amount of time, perhaps within the week, and long-term goals that take a much longer time to reach. For example, a softball player may have a short-term goal of getting a hit in a game, and a long-term goal of being the conference leader in home runs. Not all

> Goals give you something to work for, keep you in perspective, guide you to where you're going and what you need to do to get there."
>
> *- Kelly Levesque,*
> *Baylor University*

long-term goals are obtainable, but your short-term goals should be set so that you feel like you have accomplished something positive and are growing as a batter.

Set challenging yet realistic goals

Setting goals as a hitter, especially at the high school and collegiate levels, is important because it allows each hitter to set the tone for her season, to determine what goals are going to be achieved and how they are going to be achieved by the end of the season. Without setting goals, a hitter will not know what accomplishments to strive for. The goals must be realistic (challenging yet reachable) to give the hitter a purpose. If it's easy for the player to have a hit early in the game only, she could challenge herself to make her last at-bat consistently the best of the three. At every batting practice prior to the game, the hitter could work to make her last at-bats equal to the first. It may be difficult at first, but with practice it's possible to accomplish.

> I try to set a goal once a week. Depending on where I'm at and how things are going, I'll change them. If I have achieved the short-term goal, I will add a new one or modify the one I have.
>
> *- Kelly Peterson, Oregon State University*

Know what you want

If you know what you want, take the necessary steps to achieve it. For example, if your goal is to have the most RBIs in your conference, you will need to work hard and single-mindedly on being aggressive when runners are on base. Taking pride in practice to be successful in these situations rather than swinging for the fence with no purpose will allow you to be confident when runners are on base and more successful in reaching your goal. A well-thought-out goal gives the batter challenges to overcome and achievements to attain. A clear vision of where you want to end up makes it more likely that you will get there (Ravizza & Hanson, 1995).

Outcome goals

An outcome goal is the result of hitting performance, such as getting a hit, hitting a home run, putting down a bunt, or having the highest batting average on your team. Outcome goals can be easily observed and measured.

Process goals

Process goals are set to reach an outcome goal. It is what the hitter does to reach her objective. For example, if the outcome goal is to get a hit, then process goal(s) might include things such as making physical adjustments with the bat (choking up), making adjustments to the swing (pre-striding), seeing more pitches by going deeper into the count, or focusing on the pre-performance routine.

Application

Goal setting should be exercised well before any kind of performance. A common mistake made by many hitters is to set goals for games only. Goal setting is a process that begins before the season starts and should be utilized every single practice and game throughout the season. To remember your goals, write them down and review them daily. Remember that if you are struggling as a hitter and your goals are not being achieved, then the goals need to be modified. Goal setting is only beneficial when goals are being achieved. Below is a list to follow in order to organize your goal setting.

- *Before the season in the fall:* Set both short- and long-term goals, remembering that short-term goal achievement should lead to accomplishing a long-term goal, and set process and outcome goals, remembering that process goals should result in the outcome goal. See the following charts for examples.

OUTCOME Goals	PROCESS Goals
1. To get on base this at-bat	1a. Know what you want to achieve with each pitch 1b. Know the count: – ahead in count • pick pitch to swing at – behind in count • choke up • protect the plate • put ball in play 1c. Go with the pitch
2. To lay down suicide bunt	2a. Know where to place the bunt 2b. Square around early in windup 2c. Watch the pitch all the way to the bat 2d. Soften the ball/ bat contact 2e. See the ball on the ground before running to first base.

LONG-Term Goals	SHORT-Term Goals
1. Hit .300 for the season	1a. Take 50 swings at each practice 1b. Lay down 25 bunts at each practice 1c. Understand the pitching strategies of opposing pitcher(s) 1d. Define your pre-performance hitting routine 1e. Learn the umpire's strike zone 1f. Learn your coach's hitting signals
2. Have quality at-bats	2a. Begin focusing on at-bat when in the hole 2b. Rehearse swing and timing when on deck 2c. Know what you want to execute before each pitch 2d. Step out of batter's box and relax between each pitch 2e. Know the count before each pitch 2f. Know the number of outs before each pitch
3. Increase your base running speed	3a. Run a minimum of 20 sprints each practice 3b. Practice running through a base 2x/week 3c. Practice rounding a base 2x/week 3d. Practice footwork getting out of box 3x/week

- *In-season:* Monitor and make the necessary adjustments to your goals to ensure goal achievement, to make goals more challenging, or to set new ones.

For example, let's say your batting average is .150 during the first third of the season, and you've set a long-term hitting goad of .300 for the season. Is .300 realistic for you to achieve or is it beyond your skill level? If you determine that .300 is not realistic for you, then you should modify your original goal to something more reasonable (.200) and work toward that new goal. If you determine that .300 is realistic for you, then you should review your short-term goals to determine changes to them that would make a difference.

LONG-Term Goals	SHORT-Term Goals Modified
1. Hit .300 for the season	1a. Take 5̶0̶ 75 swings at each practice 1b. Lay down 2̶5̶ 50 bunts at each practice 1c. Understand the pitching strategies of opposing pitcher(s) 1d. Define your pre-performance hitting routine 1e. Learn the umpire's strike zone 1f. Learn your coach's hitting signals

- *Each practice:* Have a notebook in which your goals are written down and reviewed daily. Make a list of your hitting goals for that day's practice and after practice, rate how well/poorly you did in pursuing each goal. This list should be mostly process and short-term goals, but an outcome goal every once in a while is okay.

- *After season:* Reflect on the goals you set for yourself and rate how well/poorly you did in pursuing them.

Having a notebook with you is a great way to track your goals to see whether you are doing the things you set out to do in both practices and games. When you write down what you accomplished at practice or during the game grade yourself from 1 to 5 (1 = worked 100% at it to 5 = didn't work on it) to help you understand why you are or are not meeting your goals. If you are not meeting your goals remember to modify them to make them more realistic. This will allow you to see whether you are actually working toward your short-term goals and are consistent with your long-term goals, and whether you need to adjust the level of difficulty depending on whether you are achieving them.

Self-talk

Self-talk is defined as a "dialogue [in which] the individual interprets feelings and perceptions, regulates and changes evaluations and convictions, and gives him/herself instructions and reinforcement" (Hackfort &

Schwenkmezger, 1993). Self-talk is divided into two categories: positive and negative self-talk. Positive self-talk involves positive statements such as, "I can hit off this pitcher," "I am good at focusing on the ball," or "I am a very good ballplayer and I will succeed." Athletes who are able to engage in positive self-talk most of the time can be more successful at increasing their athletic performance. Positive self-talk results in the athlete being optimistic and more likely to learn from her mistakes rather than letting a mistake drag down her next performance. It's been shown that positive self-talk is commonly used by athletes in an attempt to improve their confidence (Gould, Hodge, Peterson & Giannini, 1989).

There was a game against Texas A&M where I had a full count during my at-bat. I said, "Ok, if it's a ball let it go," and she threw me a strike to the inside corner. I didn't swing at it and struck out. That was definitely the wrong thing to say. It wasn't necessarily negative but it was the reverse of what I should have been thinking. I should have been thinking, "See a strike, hit it." At the next at-bat, I had the same situation, same pitch. This time I told myself, "You see a strike, hit it," and I hit a home run. You learn from your mistakes, that's a big part of it. I realized after that game I had to think like an active hitter, not a passive hitter."

-Amber Hall,
University of Texas

For these reasons, negative self-talk should be avoided. Statements such as "I'll never get a hit," "I'm going to strike out," or "I hope she doesn't pitch me a change-up" hinder performance by decreasing confidence. What a player thinks often determines how she feels, and how she feels largely determines how she will play (Ravizza & Hanson, 1995). In the sport of softball, self-talk is an important factor in hitting and can set the tone for the batter to succeed or fail before she even steps into the batter's box.

Application

All individuals engage in self-talk and athletes are no exception. Self-talk is used all the time and needs to be controlled by the hitter. This is a mental skill that requires a lot of work. You must first practice identifying negative comments and turning them into positive ones. For example, a negative comment such as "Don't let your barrel drop" should be turned into a positive comment such as "Keep your barrel level." Self-talk should emphasize what you want to do, rather than what you don't want to do. There is no one particular situation in which to apply positive self-talk because self-talk is constant. You are always carrying on a conversation in your mind and there is no turning it off. Practicing self-talk should focus on making positive statements rather than negative statements. Whenever you catch yourself making a negative statement, you need to stop and replace it with a positive one. Positive self-talk should be practiced in everyday thinking with special attention to the self-talk that occurs during competition.

Pre-performance routines

Pre-performance routines are used for many different purposes, such as increasing or decreasing the athlete's arousal/anxiety level, increasing or decreasing the athlete's attention control, giving the athlete something to focus on, or giving her something to control when she doesn't feel in control of her at-bat. A pre-performance routine is the "stuff" done before the athlete is about to hit the ball. For most softball players it starts at the on-deck circle and continues as the hitter steps into the box and gets set to hit. Most hitters use a variety of technique to get them set to hit the ball. There is no single routine that all hitters should follow. It's a matter of figuring out what's comfortable for her and doing it each time she steps into the box to hit. Here are a few tips to help you understand how the pre-performance routine can improve performance.

> My pre-performance routine lets me know my tempo and allows me to focus and relax. It lets me recognize when I need to speed it up (at-bat) or slow it down. My pre-performance routine makes me feel comfortable. It's something to go to if I'm ever nervous or excited.
>
> *– Jenny Topping, 2004*
> *U.S. Olympic team*

Be Individualistic

A pre-performance routine is very individualistic. Each batter has her own list of things to do before getting ready to hit the ball. Many elite softball players engage in a variety of behaviors as part of their pre-performance routines, such as adjusting their batting gloves, licking their glove(s), gripping the bat, adjusting their helmet, taking a deep breath, making a positive self-talk statement to themselves, rearranging the dirt in the box with their feet, staring at their bat or taking exactly three swings every time. Each individual's routine can consist of one of these behaviors or combinations of them. If you think you do not have a pre-performance routine, think again, because more than likely you have one but didn't know there was a name for it.

Examples of different routines by elite softball players are provided in the pictures that follow.

1: Player A is shown getting ready to go up to bat.

2: She takes a couple of swings to get loose.

3: She receives any signals from the coach.

4: She steps into the back of the box with her right foot (left foot for lefties).

5: She measures her distance from the front of the plate.

6: She then sets up her stance, ready for the pitch.

7: *Player B is shown cleaning out the box with her feet.*

8: *She gets the signals from her coach.*

9: *She takes a couple of swings to get loose.*

10: *She stares at her bat to focus and takes a breath.*

11: *She taps the bat on the inside right foot once.*

12: *She adjusts her helmet to a fit and comfortable position.*

13: *She steps into the box and wags the bat a couple of times.*

14: *She gets into her batting stance.*

15: *She raises her bat, ready for the pitch.*

16: *Player C is shown staring at her bat and taking a breath.*

17: *She steps into the box and takes a couple of wags.*

18: *She then sets up her stance, ready for the pitch.*

Be Consistent

A pre-performance routine is kept consistent with every at-bat and between each pitch. When leaving the on-deck circle on the way to the batter's box, the hitter does her routine and gets set to hit. After every pitch (ball, strike or foul) the hitter should step out of the box, perform her entire routine, get back into the box and set for the next pitch. The routine should not change between pitches or vary in different situations, because a consistent routine helps the hitter feel more comfortable in the batter's box no matter what is going on.

Tina Boutelle stays consistent with her routine by licking her batting gloves between each pitch.

Make adjustments

If you are not comfortable with your routine (perhaps it is too long or too short), it is okay to make changes. Many hitters experiment by cutting out or adding a few deep breaths. You will find that your routine may change over time. You may not like how it is affecting you and need to make some adjustments to feel comfortable again. Make sure, though, that you are not making drastic changes all the time. Most changes should take place during practices and not during games or between at-bats. The routine should remain relatively consistent throughout the year the girls on the team or because of the coach? Did you choose a program that is good even though your playing time is questionable, or did you choose a team because you feel you will get more playing time?

The answers to these questions can help you determine the type of person you are. The answers might indicate that you may be a person who depends on getting along with other people, that you like to be by yourself, that you need a coach to motivate you, that you like to be challenged, that you're insecure concerning the unknown, etc. If you know you like challenges, then maybe you know you are a better hitter when under pressure and have a hard time getting motivated when you're not under stress. Maybe you're the type of person who doesn't perform well in pressure situations but excels when not in pressure situations. Whatever the case, you need to get to know yourself better and set realistic expectations to maintain your confidence. Below are a few questions you may want to ask to get a better understanding of yourself as a hitter and of what you need to be successful.

FINDING "ME"

1. What are my strengths and weaknesses? As you have probably played softball for a long time now, reflect on what you have been successful and unsuccessful at accomplishing as a hitter.

   I am mostly considered a:

   power hitter (clean-up hitter)   slapper (lead-off hitter)

so that you can establish a routine you like and can stick to no matter what might be happening in the game.

Use the routine to pump up or calm down

A pre-performance routine can be used to pump yourself up (increasing your arousal level) when you are not motivated or haven't been hitting well against a certain pitcher. The routine can also be used to calm down (decreasing your arousal level) when you are uptight and nervous. Rather than focusing on how nervous or uptight you are, the routine allows you to redirect your focus. The routine should not become too automatic, meaning that it should not become a habit and something you do without any thought. Each part of the routine should be deliberate and have meaning. For example, if a practice swing is part of the routine, then feel yourself taking a swing. If taking a breath is part of the routine, then feel yourself taking that breath. You have only one opportunity on each pitch and you must be ready to blast whatever the pitcher sends your way. You must be aware of your routine when you are doing it, but once you get set in the batter's box you need to redirect your focus to the ball.

Application

Implementing your pre-performance routine should become a natural part of your hitting. To get comfortable with your routine, you should always implement it:

- when hitting at practice, whether with a tee, front toss, or live pitching.

- when hitting both during a game and in the pre-game warm-up.
- when using imagery to rehearse hitting. You should visualize and feel yourself going through the routine.

THINGS TO REMEMBER:

1) Both internal and external imagery are recommended to enhance hitting performance. Imagery must be rehearsed on a consistent basis to increase recall time and vividness.

2) Set challenging but realistic goals.

3) Positive self-talk is used to improve an athlete's confidence thereby improving performance.

4) A pre-performance routine can help a hitter consistently increase her hitting performance no matter the situation.

5) Many hitters do not keep their routines exactly the same every year. One or two aspects may change based on comfort level and ease when preparing to hit.

Chapter 2
Getting to
Know "Me"

If someone were to ask you what kind of player you are, what would you say? Many softball players go through years of playing without really knowing what kind of players they are. They have not been challenged in ways other players have or put much thought into their strengths and weaknesses. Some would say they are power hitters, slappers, hard workers or leaders. Your understanding of who you are, as well as your strengths and weaknesses, can significantly improve your hitting performance.

Choosing to play at the high school or college level already provides an indication as to the type of person you may be. There are many questions you can ask yourself that can provide information to you. Why are you playing on this team? What are your contributions to this team? What do you think are your strengths and weaknesses? What do your coaches think are your strengths and weaknesses? Additional questions for college players include: Did you choose to attend a school that is far from home or did you stay close? Did you choose a school because of

I am asked to execute bunts:

    all the time   most of the time   sometimes

        once in awhile   never

I like:

    inside pitches   outside pitches   high pitches

        low pitches   change-ups

I don't like:

    inside pitches   outside pitches   high pitches

        low pitches   change-ups

I am confident batting in a game:

    always   sometimes   never

I am confident batting in practice:

    always   sometimes   never

In pressure situations I like to …

2. Motivation. What motivates me and doesn't motivate me with regard to coaches, players, opponents, my team, pressure situations, etc.

I like when my coaches …

I don't like when my coaches …

I like when my teammates …

I dislike when my teammates …

I like when my opponents …

I dislike when my opponents …

I like when my whole team …

I dislike when my whole team …

In pressure situations I like to …

In pressure situations I dislike …

3. When I am hitting well or not well, what usually happens? How do I feel?

4. Why do I play softball?

5. When I have finished my softball career, I want to be remembered as …

6. How have I grown as a hitter through these many years of playing softball?

Controllables and uncontrollables

Once you have established the type of hitter you are, you must understand which factors are within your control when hitting and which factors are not.

Controllables include those factors that you yourself can control either physically or mentally. These factors include but are not limited to:

> When I know I'm being negative I try to pick up somebody else's spirits in hopes that it will come back to me, that they will help me. It will put me back into a good place because I'm helping somebody else.
>
> — *UCLA softball player*

- *Your attitude.* The way you choose to react toward umpires' calls or fans' comments is totally up to you. You can let these occurrences affect your at-bat or you can choose to ignore them and move on. Having a positive and confident attitude will help you avoid many of the distractions you may face as a hitter.

- *Your preparation.* The amount of time you spend preparing to succeed as a hitter and the effort you put into it is under your control. You can slack off during batting practices or choose to make the most of every single pitch that comes your way. Preparation also can include getting to know your opponent. Gathering information and knowing the tendencies of your opponent will help prepare you for what is about to happen. The more you know about your opponent, the less the chance of the unexpected happening.

- *Your goals.* The goals you set as a hitter can be anything you want, from having quality at-bats to getting at least one hit a game.

Uncontrollables are the factors that are not within your control either physically or mentally. These factors include but are not limited to:

- *An umpire's call.* Whether you think a pitch is a strike or a ball is irrelevant; it is the umpire who makes the final decision, not you. A hitter must learn to accept the call and move on from there. The longer the hitter dwells on a "bad" call, the more likely the next pitch will be affected by that call.
- *The weather.* If we could control the weather, every day would be sunny. If it rains, you are not the only one who has to adjust to the situation; everyone playing has to compete in the same conditions.
- *Parents/fans.* It would be ideal if the only cheering a hitter had to deal with was positive cheering, but parents and fans often make negative comments that the hitter can hear. We wish we could control them, but they usually hoot and holler whenever they feel like it.

- *Opponents.* You can't control what a pitcher is going to pitch, or that some opponents may engage in questionable, dirty play.
- *Field conditions.* Sometimes when you step into the batter's box the dirt may be softer or harder than you are accustomed to. There might be holes from other players, forcing you to place your feet in an awkward stance. By the fourth inning at least 18 girls have kicked and dug their feet in the box. Learn to adjust and it will never be a negative factor.

To deal with uncontrollables, you must remember that while you have no control over them, you do have control over how you respond to them, in other words, your attitude. If you choose not to make an umpire's unwanted call a big deal, and you show that you are unfazed, you have won that battle. If you choose to let the un-wanted call get to you, you have lost the battle. It's hard enough trying to be confident and ready in the batter's box, so why let something that you can't control get the best of you? Play smart, be smart and be in control of your at-bat.

Emotions

Emotions can be one big reason why you hit well or hit poorly. Sometimes emotions are what makes a player who she is, for better or sometimes for worse. Have you ever had a difficult day at school or become annoyed by someone at practice and let your frustrations go into the batter's box while you were hitting? Some players would actually

> When I feel an umpire has made a bad call, it sometimes makes me angry, but I feel it makes me hit better because I get really ticked off. For some reason I feel like I need to show the umpire that he can't beat me. Since I am an extremely competitive player, any incentive is good for me.
>
> *- Carri Leto,*
> *Northwestern University*

agree that they have had this experience and have even done well hitting the softball. But not everyone does well. Each person responds to her emotions differently. Since emotions can have a significant impact on a hitter's performance, hitters need to learn to either tame their emotions or rev them up, depending on the situation when at bat. Below are a few tips to help you learn how to handle your emotions.

Tips to tame emotions during practice

If your energy is high going into or following your at-bats and you need to calm down, try these methods to turn your emotions around and give you an opportunity for improving your hitting skills:

- *3 - 2 - 1.* When working with the tee, pause to take three slow deep breaths before starting to hit. Take a cut, step back and take two more deep breaths. Take another cut, then take one long last breath. By this time you will be so focused on taking a breath and relaxing that you'll have forgotten what it was you were excited about.

- *Release.* During front toss have someone toss balls to you quickly, one after the other, forcing you to swing the bat rapidly, reload and swing again. Repeat this until you have physically vented your emotions and feel somewhat less  like the "Hulk." (This is a good substitute for breaking something and a great way to deal with anger.)

- *Power swing.* Place a basketball or soccer ball on top of a tee. For distance try to hit the ball as far as you can. Measure the distance then try to hit it farther. This is great for lowering your high energy level, and also for using your lower body to help hit the ball for power.

- *Tee focus.* Place a ball on a tee and take one power swing. Try to hit the ball as hard as you can to the other end of the batting cage. This will not only help you to focus on making solid contact with the ball, but it will also help to control your swing toward a specific target you are trying to hit. For slappers, this is like placing a ball in the 5/6 hole.

Tips to tame emotions during a game

- Be sure to use your pre-performance routine during your at-bat.
- Splash some water on your face while waiting in the dugout before you enter the on-deck circle.
- Channel your anger toward the pitcher. Pretend she told one of your teammates that you are an easy out.
- Hit off a tee. Make sure you have a tee available during the game to do some emotional releasing.
- Take some deep breaths and focus on something external, such as the ball.

Tips to rev up emotion during practice

- *Music.* Listen to some pumping-up music before you head out to practice. When you need to get excited, start singing the song that is still in your mind from before practice.

- *Challenge.* Whenever you're hitting off a tee or front toss, make up a competition with a teammate or yourself that will get you riled up during the contest. For example, if you don't hit a line drive every time, you must do five push-ups at the end of your turn or after practice.

> To release my frustration from not doing well at bat I would walk out of the dugout, walk into the bullpen, walk down to the end of the bullpen and walk back.
>
> – *Kristen Rivera,*
> *University of Washington*

- *Anger.* Find one thing that angers you most about the person front tossing or pitching live, or hang around the teammate you dislike most and interact with her. Something typically will annoy you enough to boost your energy level. If you are a person who is usually calm and needs something to get your blood flowing, this is good for a quick fix. But be warned! Sometimes you may become too pumped up when using anger as a trigger. Use it only if you benefit from it.

- *Self-talk.* Say whatever you need to say to yourself to pump yourself up. Sometimes that might even include swearing (to yourself, not out loud). You have to do what you have to do.

Tips to rev up during a game

- *Music.* Do you have a pre-game tape or an at-bat song? If your organization has the resources to provide such music, then use them. If not, carry some type of player in your bag that you can use. Pick a song that really gets you going. Remember to incorporate the music into your pre-performance routine. For example always listen to your music when in the in-the-hole position before moving to the on-deck circle. Remember that there will be times when going up to bat that your song may get played for a very short time. Be prepared and have the music ready for each at- bat. Make it count!

- *Anger.* Use the same methods to get angry during the game as in practice (described above).

- *Self-talk.* Make positive self-talk statements to yourself throughout your at-bat. Look for the good in every situation and pat yourself on the back for that good thing.

THINGS TO REMEMBER:

1) Not all tips will work. As discussed earlier, each person is different, and what other players do to get themselves pumped up or calmed down is their thing. Just because one thing works for you doesn't mean that all of them will. Some may work better for other players.

2) Take these tips and individualize them. If you would like to revise the 3-2-1 method to make it a 1-2-3 method, do it! If it works for you, then it's what you should be doing. No one can tell you what you should or shouldn't do, but knowing what other players do might help you and has helped other players in the past. Hopefully by reading these tips you can perhaps even create your own methods. The buck doesn't stop here.

3) Learning about yourself is a continuous process that should be revisited every now and then. As you start your softball career, continue it or wind it down, you should understand yourself as a hitter more and more each day, and reorganize the strides you have made to get you where you are today. The most important person in your life is you, so get to love and appreciate who you are.

Chapter 3
Practice vs. Game

The problem

Many players have a hard time applying what they learn and rehearse in practice to game situations. At practice players can easily:

- have confidence going into the box (not be afraid to hit off a certain pitcher, put the bunt down, or have runners on base with two outs in the seventh inning);
- execute when asked to put a bunt down, hit a sacrifice fly or move a runner over;
- have quality at-bats (let balls go by, swing at strikes, foul off balls, be a hard out, have a plan, be prepared);
- hit well (hit home runs or line drives)

The fact of the matter is that when it comes to a game, many players have a harder time performing than in practice. Many practices are designed to rehearse a particular play over and over again. The athletes know exactly what is about to happen, so they do not have to utilize their decision-making skills. However in a game the athlete must perceive the situation, analyze it, decide what action to take, and then perform that action. Decision making needs to be rehearsed during practice, not just left to game situations.

Differences

Pressure is common during a game but rarely present at practice. Coaches typically work hard to make practices free from stress and to emphasize learning rather than mistakes. It's okay if you fail to execute during practice because there will be practice again tomorrow and statistics are not being kept.

It's a whole different story in a game. There is no room for making errors or not executing. A mistake in a game can have a profound impact. This is the place where the hitter must be prepared to perform and execute when needed. After a poor execution, athletes may have an "I don't know how to execute anymore" crisis. This crisis can last a day or two, a week, or possibly the whole season based on the importance of the game and the situation. This is the time for a hitter's mental skills to kick in, and the hitters who are better at turning it around will have a shorter "crisis" to deal with. The hitters who do not use the mental game may prolong the crisis. The key to hitting in both practice and games is for the hitter to build confidence to execute whatever is asked of her.

Below are some important differences between practices and games that can explain why a hitter's performances vary in those two situations.

Practice

- Practice can last up to four hours a day and provides many opportunities to execute.
- The time a player individually spends on hitting varies, and she can swing numerous times (live hitting, tee work, front toss).
- A player goes through many hitting repetitions.
- The hitter has an idea of where the pitches are that are being pitched to her.
- If she makes a mistake she can try again right away.
- The hitter has the option of working on whatever she wants to (outside pitches, change-ups, etc.).
- There usually is no count or score.
- There are no umpires or fans to distract the hitter.
- The player usually plays on the same field.

Games

- A game can last from one-and-a-half to three hours.
- The time the player individually spends on hitting can range from 10 seconds to five minutes, depending on the number of at-bats and number of pitches per at-bat.
- The hitter can have about 20 – 40 minutes between each at-bat.

- If the hitter messes up (strikes out, misses a bunt and run, etc.) she may not be able to try again.
- The hitter must adjust to what the pitcher is pitching her and execute with that pitch.
- The hitter doesn't know what pitch she may be getting.
- There is a count and score to the game which influences the player's hitting.
- The hitter has to adjust to the umpire.
- The hitter must execute whatever and whenever the coach asks her to execute.
- The hitter is familiar with the skills of the opposing pitcher, which may help or hinder a hitter's performance.
- There's additional pressure and anxiety from fans, family and friends watching and evaluating the hitter's performance.
- Games are played at different fields and stadiums with different atmospheres.

Mindset

Practice is a time when you can focus on how good a softball hitter you want to be. What you do mentally during hitting practice is up to you. Below are some tips you can always use to help you mentally approach hitting at practice:

- If you want practice to be game-like, then practice as if it were a game. During practice, you hit the ball, hit the ball, and hit the ball, usually with no pause between pitches or tosses. But in a game you pause between each pitch and have an umpire calling balls and strikes. If you can make every practice hitting situation as game-like as possible, you will become more prepared to face the real game situation.

- Practice quality, not quantity. From the time you begin hitting off a tee or receiving a front toss, take the time and effort to make quality swings. Quality means each swing should be thought out and made with 100 percent effort. Many times batters will hit off a tee and take 30 cuts. Out of the 30 cuts maybe only 10 were swings for which the batter took her time, focused and executed how she wanted to hit them. For the other 20 swings she hurried, was not as focused, and put little effort into them. Some steps to ensure that you have quality at-bats are:

Have a plan

Whether you are working on a tee, front toss or live, figure out what you want to accomplish during that particular practice session. It could be hitting line drives; working on outside pitches, inside pitches or change-ups; adjusting your weight balance, your stride or your hand speed; taking your time between each pitch; being aggressive, etc. When you have decided what you are going to work on keep it consistent for the day, or longer if necessary.

Take your time

Rushing through your tee work or front toss does not maximize hitting performance. Taking your time will help you evaluate each swing and allow you to make the necessary adjustments for the next swing. Have you ever experienced an at-bat where you were out in less than five seconds without knowing what happened? It's probably because you rushed between pitches and didn't give any thought to what was happening with each pitch. Ask yourself this question: If a pitcher rushes you in the box and tries to quick pitch, do you like it? If your answer is no, then don't do it to yourself. Try it! Rush through a round of front tosses and compare your performance to when you

If you are hitting live, take the time to go through an at-bat as you would in a game.

take your time maximizing each pitch. Most hitters agree that the latter leads to better performance.

Give each swing all your focus and effort. Be absorbed in what you are doing. If you're going to take the time to put a ball on a tee, have a coach front toss to you or be pitched to, give your swing the utmost focus and energy. Focus means blocking out all the distractions — teammates, fans, opponents, to name a few. When you are set and ready to swing, nothing but pounding the softball should be on your mind. Effort means taking a full swing. Not swinging out of your shoes, but with control and a purpose. Would you want to go up to bat in a game and take half swings? Absolutely not! So don't do it in practice. If you are going to take a cut at the ball, do it knowing that you gave all you had at that moment. This will make even those bad pitches you swung at seem like good pitches, because you swung with conviction and increased your chances of a successful outcome.

Positive ttitude

Be happy to be a part of your team and to have the opportunity to go to practice every day. Sometimes being with your team 24/7 can take its toll, but remember it is only for a small period of time compared to your whole life. Take pride in your hitting, pride that you make everything the best you possibly can at that moment. You can hit every pitch, you are the hardest worker hitting off

the tee, front toss and live pitching. You love being challenged or questioned about your hitting because you know you can prove them wrong. You work on your weaknesses to make them strengths. You listen to criticism from other players and coaches and decide whether or not it applies to you. It's this attitude that will separate you from the other hitters on your team and from other teams. It's the constant desire to improve that will get you through the practices that seem long and tiring. You can leave practice every day knowing that you did all you could do to improve as a hitter.

Physical adjustments

Below are some things that you can do physically to make your hitting at practice more game-like.

- *Follow your pre-performance routine.* During practice go through your pre-performance routine just as you would in a game. During the pregame warm-up tee work, front toss and/or live pitching, take one swing at a time and simulate the game (i.e., step out of the box as you would in a game then return ready for the next swing or pitch). If you have a long pre-performance routine, don't go through it every time; once every so often should be sufficient. Try creating a shorter version for practice when you don't have the space or time to execute the long routine. For example, if your long pre-performance routine is to step out of the box, tighten your batting gloves, take two swings, take your breath and get back in the box, you could try instead to step out of the box, take a breath and get back in.

- *Don't take one more.* If you are switching through stations and happen to end poorly, don't take another swing. Challenge yourself to end badly and take that feeling to the next station. This will challenge you to turn around your at-bat and to deal with frustration that might build up. In a game sometimes your at-bats don't go your way — perhaps you strike out — and you have to carry your frustration to the next at-bat or another game. Work at being comfortable with being uncomfortable. In other words, don't let the feeling of being uncomfortable be strange to you. If you practice dealing with being uncomfortable, it will give you the confidence to battle through it.

- *Work on your focusing abilities.* Have a tape of your fans, teammates and coaches cheering for you during your at-bat and telling you things to do. Play

Simulating your team cheering as they would in a game can help you prepare for the real thing when it happens.

this tape while you are working on a tee or front toss. The tape will make your experience almost real. This will help you determine whether or not you are focused. If you can hear what your team-mates and coaches are saying, you know that you need to focus more on the pitch.

- *Master your negative self-talk.* If you are having a hard time blocking out the negative comments you tell yourself when you are hitting poorly, make a tape of them. Play the tape while you are hitting, so you can work on blocking out your own distractions.

- *Visualize.* Visualize yourself in a bases-loaded situation, in a seventh inning game-winning at-bat, as a lead-off hitter of the inning, or in a bunt-and-run situation. Play out the at-bats as you would in a game.

- *Spark competition.* Grab a partner and challenge her to a competitive match. Have your front toss or live pitcher call out the signal to perform a certain task, or set a certain situation and allot points for each execution. The person with the most points wins. To raise the stakes, add washing a car or buying a soda to the winnings. Adding stress and competitiveness to the challenges will hopefully simulate the emotions you feel in a game.

THINGS TO REMEMBER:

1) Applying the good hitting executed during practice into a game takes practice and confidence that you are prepared to succeed.

2) A game differs from practice in that the anxiety you put upon yourself is greater and the time between each at-bat is longer.

3) Making practice more game-like and having quality at-bats and a positive attitude are the first steps toward transitioning your successes from practice into the game.

4) Be comfortable with feeling uncomfortable.

Chapter 4
Facing a
Dominant Pitcher

Mindset

When you find yourself facing a dominant pitcher who overpowers you as a hitter, it can get discouraging. You must control how you mentally approach that pitcher. Below are some tips to help change your mindset when facing a dominant pitcher.

- *You define the dominant pitcher.* You as the hitter should define for yourself what a dominant pitcher is. She could be a pitcher who pitches fast or slowly, gets the hitter to chase balls, has good composure (shows no emotion), pitches to her strengths and not the hitter's weakness, strikes out hitters, or gets ahead early in the count. Whatever the case may be, a dominant pitcher is different for every hitter.

- *Approach the pitcher as if you have nothing to lose.* Since the pitcher is known for being fast and/or striking out hitters, the hitter striking out is the expected result. You should realize that this is a great opportunity to become an improved hitter. Yes, you may be frustrated from striking out or not getting a hit, but getting a hit should not be the goal you want to set for yourself against a dominant pitcher. Your goal should be to have quality at-bats and give yourself every possible opportunity for some kind of success.

- *Reverse your mindset* so that you are the dominating hitter and the pitcher is afraid to face you. Reverse the roles!

- *Set a reasonable strategy for yourself.* Because a hit is not always within the complete control of the hitter, you should focus on a strategy you can accomplish. As a hitter you should understand that the only way to be successful is to stay confident and take your at-bat one pitch at a time. Learn to focus on the little things. Some strategies include:
    - Going after the first two pitches. Great pitchers will always try to get ahead in the count with

the first and second pitch. This allows them to mess around with you after that first strike by pitching you balls or change-ups. If her first pitch isn't a strike, you can definitely guess the second one will be.

– Working your routine. When you approach the batter's box, remember that the pitcher is pitching *for* you. It is your box and your at-bat. If the pitcher is taking too long or pitching too fast, call time and get out of the box until you are ready. *You* control the at-bat. This is a great chance for you to take your breath between pitches and refocus for each pitch. Stay consistent with your routine because it's something you can always go back to after every pitch when you feel you have no control of your at-bat. Nobody can take your routine away from you. It's what you use to calm yourself down or pump yourself up for the next pitch.

– Battling during your at-bats. You must go up to bat intending to be a difficult out. Many batters will face a dominant pitcher and end up being an easy out. In other words, the pitcher is not worried about pitching to you. Go up to bat with the attitude that you will not give up, no matter what. Take strong swings but don't swing out of your shoes. Swing with a purpose, as if you

liked that pitch. When you battle you foul off
the balls, bring the count to a full count and do
everything necessary to extend your at-bat and
make the pitcher work. Look to take advantage
of any pitching mistake. Even dominant pitchers don't always hit their spots, and when they
don't, you'll be ready to hit the ball hard.

–   Using relevant information. Know the pitcher's
    pitches ahead of time. Use this knowledge in
    your pregame warm-up to mentally prepare for
    what is coming. Watch your teammates' at-bats;
    know the pitcher's go-to pitch. Is there a pitch

she likes to use most of the time? Does she seem easily frustrated? Use these little bits of information to help you and your teammates. After the first couple of batters, tell the rest of the line-up what pitches you are seeing, whether or not they have much movement, and how the umpire is calling the strike zone. Catchers can also provide this information to the hitters. Communication between teammates can help everyone.

Physical adjustments

These are some physical adjustments that can improve your chances of succeeding when facing a dominant pitcher.

During practice:

- Practice hitting off faster pitches by speeding up the machine or moving the pitcher closer to the plate to make the speed less intimidating. If you gain experience with the fast pitching during practice, it won't surprise you come game time.

- Practice hitting drills that work on a quicker swing and provide a good look at the faster ball.

- Have someone toss the ball from the catcher's position to the front of the batter. The batter must try to hit it.
- Have someone drop the ball (head high) in front of the batter where she would normally make contact. The batter then must try to hit the ball before it drops to the ground.
- Side toss two different-colored balls up at the batter and call out which ball she must hit.
- Lower your bat head a bit to make it more horizontal to the ground in order to reduce the time it takes to swing at a fastball.

- Put your imagination to work when hitting off the tee. Imagine the pitcher you are facing and put yourself into a variety of worst case scenarios, such as having a count of two strikes, no balls.

- Work at-bats with front toss, machine or tee. Work at not being frustrated. If you are frustrated keep battling, because the more you practice on turning around your frustrations, the easier it will be when the game comes.

- Choke up on your bat when working with higher speeds. This will give you much more control on your bat and a better chance to make contact with the ball.

- Pre-stride or have no stride at all. Pre-striding means stepping before the pitcher pitches the ball so that

When you experience faster pitching or are behind in the count, choke up on the bat to increase your chances of putting the ball in play.

you can have a faster swing and your weight is balanced. Having no stride at all means not taking a step. This also minimizes the time it will take for you to hit the ball. This must be practiced constantly so that it doesn't feel odd. Strive to find your comfort level!

During pregame:

- Pre-stride/no stride.
- Choke up on the bat.
- Use imagery of the pitcher.
- Work fast pitches and those the opposing pitcher is good at pitching.
- Lower the head of the bat to reduce its swing path.

During the game:

- Pre-stride/no stride.
- Choke up on the bat.
- Work your routine. Slow down the at-bat to your pace. Take your time, don't let the pitcher rush you, and remember that you control each at-bat.
- Lower the head of the bat to reduce its swing path.

THINGS TO REMEMBER:

1) You must continually make adjustments and prepare to succeed.

2) Minimize nonquality at-bats to maximize opportunity. This means working on positive thinking and making adjustments, such as releasing your poor at-bat frustrations and refocusing on the task at hand.

3) Find confidence in the small things (i.e., making adjustments during the at-bat, keeping quality in perspective, going to bat giving it your all). Give yourself the best possible chance to succeed.

Chapter 5
Facing a Non-dominant Pitcher

Mindset

When you find yourself getting overpowered by a non-dominant pitcher, it can be just as frustrating as facing a dominant pitcher. On many occasions hitters will face pitchers who just don't pitch well. Maybe the type of pitches she can throw is limited or she just isn't consistent with strikes. In return the hitter may not be challenged to want to hit well off of her. This can lead to an unmotivated, poor performance by the hitter. Below are some tips to change the hitter's mindset when facing a nondominant pitcher.

- *Who is a nondominant pitcher?* You as the hitter should define for yourself what a nondominant pitcher is. She could be a pitcher who pitches slow or wild balls, walks many batters, hits batters, throws pitches over the plate, or can't pitch for more than three innings in a game before being removed. Whatever the case may be, defining a nondominant pitcher is different for every hitter.

- *Poor pitching does not equal hits.* Just because a pitcher is notorious for not doing her job well doesn't mean you'll have an easy time hitting off of her. Many times top-level teams face opponents who don't have dominating pitching but fail to hit as well as they usually do. This is because the hitters don't give much value or effort to the at-bats or they become impatient to hit rather than taking a walk. Has there ever been a time when you faced a poor pitcher and came out of it unsuccessful and frustrated? Just because the pitcher isn't dominant doesn't mean the hitter is guaranteed a hit.

> The nondominant pitcher is sometimes the hardest to face because you train yourself so much to be precise and to look for a particular pitch that you get caught off guard when they throw it down the middle. Sometimes it's too fast and you're so shocked that it's there that you think, "I should be crushing this girl," but you're not. That in itself can be frustrating.
>
> *-Aimee Minor,*
> *University of Washington*

- *Become familiar with the opposing pitching staff.* If you know you are going to face a team that has poor pitching, use the internet or media guide to acquaint yourself with these pitchers. See what they look like and what they have done in the past as well as how they are doing now. Ask your coaches if they have videotape of the pitchers from prior meetings. The reason to study the pitchers is to add meaning and familiarity of them to your at-bats. You will be excited and look forward to facing this opponent if you know who and what this opponent can do. It's similar to getting excited about facing a dominant pitcher you know and wanting another crack at her pitching.

- *Keep your at-bats the same.* Now that you have become familiar with the pitcher and you are motivated to hit against her, make sure your focus isn't solely on who she is. Stick with your at-bat routine and change nothing. Go with the same mindset you use when facing a dominant or average pitcher. Just because you may do a little extra homework to get motivated for a particular opponent doesn't mean you should change your normal routine or goals for your at-bats.

Some strategies to think about when facing a nondominant pitcher include:

- *Be a little more cautious.* Nondominating pitchers often tend to pitch more balls. Since they are usually the type of pitcher who doesn't hit their spots well, don't expect every first pitch to be a strike. More than likely you will see a strike by the second or third pitch, or maybe not at all.

- *Be patient.* Many hitters are seen hacking away at pitches that are thrown for balls by this type of pitcher. Since nondominant pitchers usually tend to pitch more balls than strikes, make sure that you are swinging at strikes only. Don't get so impatient that you swing at balls trying to get a hit rather than taking a walk.

- *Work on your weaknesses.* If you know that you are impatient with slower, junk ball pitchers, make sure you spend time preparing for the encounter. A quick adjustment that can help against this type of pitcher is to stay back in the pre-stride/no stride. Make sure that on the tee, front toss or live, you work on staying back on change-ups and balls.

- *Work on your takes.* This means watching a pitch go by and not swinging at it. Make sure that when you take a ball, you haven't given up your weight to the front foot; in other words, you haven't shifted your

weight forward. If you find yourself shifting your weight, you will have a hard time hitting those pitches that are slower or heading in a different direction than you expect. If you can take a step and have a take without giving up your weight, you will have the pitcher's number and be ready for whatever she will throw you. Holding the weight back also keeps the power in your swing. By doing this you can avoid those missed swings, pop-ups or dinky grounders.

THINGS TO REMEMBER:

1) Facing a nondominant pitcher does not necessarily mean having easy pitches to hit. Most of the time these pitchers are more difficult to hit against.

2) Study the tendencies of the opposing pitcher you might face to motivate yourself to hit against her.

3) Nondominant pitchers are known for throwing more balls than strikes, so be a patient hitter and wait for your strike.

Chapter 6
Life as a
Designated Hitter

The designated hitter (DH) role is probably one of the toughest positions mentally in the sport of softball. The DH position is best described as a player who "only" hits. What makes this position so mentally difficult is the fact that if she doesn't execute as a hitter, she has no other way to contribute to the team's performance. She doesn't play defense and has only approximately three at-bats per game to prove herself as a hitter. The goal of the DH is to get a hit and get on base. Many times coaches will reserve the DH role for the power hitter. Typically the power hitter can hit the long ball or make a significant impact with one swing of the bat. Anyone taking on the role of a DH should understand five mental characteristics needed for this role. These include understanding the stressors or negative aspects, the positive aspects, the expectations, the mindset and the physical preparation associated with the DH role.

Stressors/negative aspects associated with the DH role

There are many stressors or negative aspects that the designated hitter must deal with when hitting in this position. A stressor or negative aspect can include anything that causes mental or physical strain. They are individualistic and are perceived differently by different hitters. Some common stressors and negative aspects for those in the DH role include:

- *Pressure to perform well at every at-bat.* Because the DH's role is to get a hit, many times the DH feels an obligation to get a hit every time she steps up to bat. This obligation comes from the fact that there is only one hitter on the team in this role. Designated hitters have a tendency to perceive a lot of pressure during each at-bat and therefore try "too" hard. This added pressure increases arousal and anxiety which results in decreased hitting performance.

> When you're not doing well as a DH it's hard not to think about whether your coach will replace you or not. But at the same time it can motivate you to do whatever it takes to get on base, whether it's walking, or even taking one for the team (getting hit by the pitch).
>
> – Cassie Morales,
> Syracuse University

- *Feeling easily replaceable.* The DH position is a very difficult one because the player in it is easily replaceable. If she is not hitting there are about four other teammates who are not yet playing that the coach can substitute for her. This substitution would not interfere with the defensive line-up. If her replacement does poorly, there is always somebody next in line.

- *Staying focused.* Since the DH is not playing defensively, she may have the tendency not to be fully involved in the game. She has plenty of time to talk to other players in the dugout, eat seeds, sit on the bench, and check out the stands to see who has come to the game today. When all she does is hit, it is

very hard to stay focused, motivated and involved in the game. But the DH must stay involved when her team goes out to play defense. For example, when there are runners on base the DH must be alert for the defense to call out when she is stealing. Staying involved during defense will also make her aware of what she will need to perform well in the game.

Positive aspects associated with the DH role

Even though there are many stressors and negative aspects involved with being a DH, there are also many positive aspects to the position. Some of these include:

- *Focusing on one thing.* The DH doesn't have to worry about playing defense. Since the DH's only role is to hit, the DH only needs to focus on the opposing pitcher.

- *Time to think about her at-bat.* If the DH happens to be the last out or on base when the opposing team gets three outs, she has time to return to the dugout and reflect on the previous at-bat and the adjustments that are needed the next time. Defensive position players do not have this time to reflect nor should they be reflecting on their last at-bat. They must grab their gloves and quickly sprint out to their defensive positions while switching into fielding mode.

- *The chance to show potential.* Most coaches will find a defensive fielding position for a DH if the DH is hitting more consistently than the full-time starters. This provides an opportunity for the DH to play defensively. If she hits better than the majority of the position players and can hang defensively with them, it may give her the opportunity to become a starter if one of the position players begins to hit poorly.

Force the pitcher to continue throwing pitches — it only takes one poorly pitched ball to force the action.

Expectations associated with the DH role

There are many expectations that a designated hitter must learn to live with but at the same time not fall victim to. DH expectations must be challenging yet realistic. If all the other hitters expect to get a hit once every three at-bats (for a batting average of .333), why then should the DH be expected to get a hit every at-bat? Hits are nice, but almost as effective is being able to produce what the offensive situation calls for at that particular moment, such as a bunt, a hit and run, or a sacrifice fly.

- Be aggressive and make things happen when at bat.
- Be a threat to the defense every time you step into the batter's box.
- Be able to execute any signal given by the coach.
- Be flexible (if taken out, be supportive and understanding of the coach's decision).
- Be ready to go in to hit at any time.
- Be supportive of the defensive players on the field.

Mindset associated with the DH role

A DH must understand a few mental aspects associated with her role if she wants to be mentally successful as a DH. Some of these mental aspects include the following:

- *Take pride in the DH role.* The DH falls into a category of players that is expected to make a positive impact every time she has an at-bat. It takes more than just getting a hit to be a good DH. It takes an understanding of what the DH's role is on the team and how she chooses to embrace it. Everything she does during practice and a game should be in preparation to succeed in any situation. When someone asks her what position she plays, or announces it over the loud speaker, she should lift her chin high with conviction and heart that she is a *designated hitter*. She should never feel ashamed of her role, thinking that she won't ever be a position player. She has been chosen to face a battle that many players can't handle mentally.

- *Be prepared for anything.* At any given time the coach can put the DH into a game. It could be her sole role for the entire game or she could go in for one at-bat. Many times if a particular batter has not been hitting well and a crucial situation arises, the coach will call a time-out and put in the DH to make the

A DH can be asked to do anything, so be prepared to execute everything.

game-winning hit. She should expect to go in to hit at the most nerve-racking, nail-biting moments, to turn the game around. She should make sure that she is prepared for these situations and is ready to do some damage.

> G ame preparation to me is the most important thing in hitting. The difference between the good players and the great is how they individually prepare. If a player can control her preparation and emotions and be ready for every single game and practice, she already has the battle won.
>
> – *Jenny Topping, 2004*
> *U.S. Olympic team*

- *The DH can't always do it all.* She can't always get a hit, even though she knows her coach wants her to. The DH is a very difficult role, in that she always gets put into the game at the most crucial moments. She should remember, though, like everybody else, she will get many more chances to shine. The most important thing is to have quality at-bats and be confident every time she goes up to bat. If she's nervous she shouldn't show it. She must step into the batter's box looking like she has this pitcher in the bag. *Sometimes the DH must fake it to make it.*

Physical preparation for the DH role

Here are some tips that can help the DH succeed in physically preparing to become a better, more consistent designated hitter.

During practice:

- Work on your pre-performance routine, because you will definitely need it for all those nail-biting situations you will find yourself in.
- Use imagery during batting practice by creating stressful situations in your mind.
- Work the at-bats by pretending that you are hitting in a game and must execute your plan during that at-bat.

When your team is on defense:

- Work off a tee since you have the luxury of rehearsing your hitting more than the defensive players.

When your team is on offense:

- Study the opposing pitcher to find the go-to pitch the pitcher throws when she gets behind in the count.
- Study your own hitters, observing the pitches that most of the batters are failing to hit or are chasing.
- Get information from hitters who have already faced the pitcher. Don't wait until you are put in the game to ask. Be more ready than anyone else on the team.

THINGS TO REMEMBER:

1) Have pride in your role as the designated hitter.

2) Though there are some negative aspects of being a DH, there are many positive ones also.

3) Be prepared for your coach to put you in at any time in the game. Expect to be put in at the most crucial times!

Study the pitcher as she pitches to your teammates.

Chapter 7
The Highs and
Lows of Hitting

Hitting Streaks

A hitting streak occurs when a hitter performs successfully game after game. The hits are linked from game to game without interruption. For example someone may say, "That girl is on a 10-game hitting streak," meaning for 10 straight games she has had a hit.

Obtaining and maintaining a streak

A streak can be obtained, but not if a batter is striving for it. Usually hitters can obtain it when they are more focused on the process (having a plan, feeling confident, working their routine, etc.) than on getting a hit. More than likely a hitter is not even aware of being in a hitting streak, and when they do realize it, it usually ends. The hitter becomes nervous that she might ruin the streak and possibly tries too hard to keep the streak going. It is difficult to maintain a hitting streak, but a hitter can increase her odds of getting consistent hits by working on her process and staying confident rather than by focusing on getting hits.

What hitters think about

Players in a hitting streak sometimes feel like they are in the "zone." In other words, they are so involved with the at-bat that they have no distractions, no worries, and execute the hit with ease. Most of the time, when a batter

is doing well and you ask them, "What were you thinking of?" they will say, "Nothing." The feeling is unexplainable. It's similar to watching television and getting sucked into a show so much that you are not aware of the people around you and are not thinking about anything. You are just enjoying the show. When a hitter is up to bat in the "zone," they are paying attention to the pitcher and only the pitcher. No outside distractions interfere with the process of hitting.

Adjusting to praise

Have you ever heard someone warn, "If you ever wanted to ruin how well a hitter is hitting, tell them"? The reason a hitter's performance will decline is because she will start thinking about her hitting and get worried about maintaining it. More than likely she will focus on how well she is doing rather than on what she is doing. It's similar to your coach telling you, "Don't pop up," and all you think about is popping up. If somebody ever tells you how well you are hitting, big deal. You have to say to yourself, "Yeah I am doing well, but so what? I worked hard and earned it." If you go through a hitting streak, enjoy it. Not many hitters can hit in multiple games for a period of time. You may clap four times but not five, because one more might blur your focus and force you to lose track of what you are really trying to accomplish (to improve your performance). In other words, be happy when you are doing well, but don't cheer about it too much or the next thing you know, you'll lose focus and start hitting poorly.

> When I am in the box, I don't hear anything. My teammates do certain cheers and ask me whether I can hear them, I tell them no. When I'm out of the box I can hear them and also my parents, but as soon as I put one foot in the box I can't hear anything.
>
> *- Carri Leto,*
> *Northwestern University*

Slumps

Some players define a slump as not getting a hit in two games, while others define a slump as not getting a hit in four games. A slump is something that is set and defined by the individual. You may think that a slump is not getting a hit during one game, while a teammate might think a slump is not hitting for an entire tournament. A slump shouldn't be linked to getting hits. Quality at-bats should be viewed as successful at-bats. Players also feel compelled to compare their present performance with those of previous years. For example, if a hitter hit .400 during her freshman year with 20 home runs, and during her sophomore year hit .340 with 10 home runs, she may consider herself to be in a slump even though on average her performance can be considered pretty good. The reason for this "slump-mode thinking" is based on the standards you set for yourself as a hitter. If you are the type of person who demands a lot from yourself and expects to get a hit at every at-bat, you will more likely feel like you are in a slump after not executing. If you are the type of person who is not too critical of yourself, it may take four to five hitless games before you feel that you are in a slump.

When you are in a slump, you feel as if this is the worst

hitting performance you have had in your hitting career. You feel as if you are in a deep hole and can't get out. Assuming the cause behind a slump is not technical, here are some tips to help get you back to hitting the ball well.

- *What's off?* Find out what is causing you not to hit. Have you changed your normal practice and pre-game routines or shifted the focus of your results and goals? How about mentally? What has your thought process been like? Have you been positive or negative? How about your at-bats? Could it be the pitches you are swinging at? Or might it be something physical, such as dropping your bat head or getting jammed? You may not be able to figure out exactly what is wrong, but you should have some idea as to what you could work on.

- *Focus on the little things.* Getting out of a slump takes time and patience. You can't expect to get over a slump in one day. Many times hitters can have two to three slumps a season. The key to getting out of a slump and back on track is to stop worrying about the slump and focus on the little things. Take the extra time at practice to work with your coach on your mechanics, work off the tee, and work on being confident in the box and having quality at-bats.

- *All about the process.* Paying attention to the little things will help you to focus on the process, not the outcome. Throughout the book we have emphasized the importance of focusing on the process because that is what sets up the outcome. If your goal is to get a hit, then work on hitting a ball, adjusting to pitches, and not letting anyone or anything distract you during your at-bat. You must work hard at the little goals to give yourself the best opportunity to succeed at the bigger ones.

- *Stay positive.* Having a positive mindset will greatly increase your chances of getting out of a slump. Sometimes it's the negative attitude that can get you into the slump in the first place. You have probably noticed that sometimes before an at-bat, you do not feel certain you are going to get a hit. The only thing you are certain of (in your mind) is that one hit will end your slump and end the "curse" of not being able to get a hit. If you do not get a hit, you go back to the negative attitude, "Oh great, I'm getting worse and worse as a hitter," or "I couldn't hit anything if my life depended on it." You must

A batting slump is like the rain – it eventually ends and the sun comes out!

turn this around and realize you have nothing to lose. The situation could not be any worse and it can only get better from there. Having a positive attitude and using positive self-talk, such as "I will hit off her," or "I can't wait to get another chance to hit," will have a positive impact on the next at-bat.

Getting out of a slump is probably one of the hardest things to do, because you know when you are in a slump and only you know what it will take to get out of it. You have to realize that hitting consistently well at every game is an impossible goal to maintain. If you happen not to hit for a while so what? Don't worry about the slump any more than you do a strike-out. There will be more at-bats, practices and games to improve your hitting and to work on your process. Remember, there is more to a successful at-bat than getting a hit.

Sometimes however, the hitter may reach a point when she has tried everything to get out of a slump and yet nothing seems to work. She has worked on the little things, focused on her routine, taken many breaths to relax, and set goals to achieve, but nothing seems to be working. Some of the above suggestions will help to end a slump but they may not necessarily work all the time for every hitter. In most cases seeking help outside the softball team can work.

Here are a couple of suggestions that have helped players in the past when none of the mental skills were working for them.

- *Miracle workers.* When your coach doesn't seem to be making any sense and your teammates think they all know the answers, go to somebody else for advice. Many times talking to your parents, an old batting coach or friends about how you're feeling and asking for a solution from them can help. Sometimes hearing it from somebody you look up to and respect will help you find the answer. They may be giving you the same advice your coaches and teammates are giving you, but hearing it from someone else can be quite refreshing.

- *Be realistic.* Sometimes batters get so caught up in hitting that they feel it's the end of the world when they are not hitting well. But when it comes down to it, it's not the end of the world. There are worse problems such as disease, death and dropping out of school that are much more important than not hitting a softball. Keep your hitting in perspective. It's just a game, and there are millions of people who

Keep your head up, it's not the end of the world if you're not hitting well right now. Everyone has a slump sooner or later.

don't even know you're playing it. Ask yourself this question: You have only a limited number of years in your life to play softball. Do you really want to waste that time being frustrated because you are having a hard time hitting? Probably not, so take hitting for what it's worth and don't let yourself be too bummed about not being able to hit a ball all the time.

THINGS TO REMEMBER:

1) A hitting streak cannot be controlled, and is only a result of the hard work you put into your process.

2) Slumps are determined individually by a player. They depend on the standards you set for yourself as a hitter.

3) When nothing seems to work, you can go to parents or friends for help or a solution. Hearing advice from someone outside the softball team can sometimes help.

Chapter 8
Success & Failure
are Feedback

Feedback

Feedback (FB) is one of the most important contributions to the success of a softball hitter: There are two types of FB; intrinsic FB and extrinsic FB. Intrinsic FB is the feedback your body senses send you. For example, if you take a swing and get jammed you can hear an unusual sound and feel the shock given by the contact of the ball on the handle of the bat through your hands. Extrinsic FB is when you receive the feedback from somebody else or from something other than your senses. Most hitters rely extensively on intrinsic FB but should also use extrinsic FB. A coach or a teammate might see something with your swing or approach in the box that you don't notice or feel. Listening to what other people have to say can give you many different perspectives as to why or how you could improve your hitting. Deciding which feedback to embrace and which to disregard is the tricky part.

Sources of extrinsic feedback

In order to benefit from other people's views on how you are doing as a hitter, you must be willing to listen. You must not take criticism personally and angrily. Understand that people may not always be good at communicating their opinions in a kind and understanding manner. But remember that feedback from other people is better than no FB at all.

Common sources of extrinsic FB include coaches, teammates and parents. Basically these are the people who most often watch you hit. Here are some thoughts on the extrinsic FB given by these people and whether it might be of help to you with your hitting:

- *Coaches.* Coaches are by far the best source for identifying what is right and wrong with your swing. It is their job to find the faults in players' swings and most have a lot of experience doing so. They want you to succeed as a hitter and want to help you in

Coaches watch EVERY-THING.

any way they can. Remember, coaches watch every pitch during every one of your at-bats.

Listen to what a coach tells you, because they can see the whole picture.

- *Teammates.* Your fellow teammates are another great source of extrinsic FB on your hitting. However you may have only two or three teammates who follow your style of hitting and can tell if you are doing something different. Others are probably too busy paying attention to what the pitcher is pitching, or talking among themselves, etc. So it's important for a hitter to identify

Teammates can provide you with valuable hitting information.

which teammates (if any) know your swing well enough to provide useful FB.

- *Parents*. Parents can also be a good source of extrinsic FB, depending on their knowledge and experience with hitting. Your parents will be the first to give you truthful, straightforward advice, even if it is something you don't want to hear. Usually the FB people don't want to hear is very close to the truth, so you should use it to your advantage. Your mom and dad have been with you your whole life and can probably tell whether you're stressed during an at-bat or whether something is off-beat in your swing. They can also bring a new perspective to your at-bat. They will always be the first to let you know that it's okay if you didn't perform well; they still love you and were happy to watch you play.

CAUTION- Even though the three groups of people mentioned above are good sources of extrinsic FB, that doesn't mean you should do everything they say. You may come to realize that some of their FB isn't useful or doesn't apply to you, and that's okay. You shouldn't completely disregard the FB; just take the time to figure out what is helpful and whether you can apply it in the future.

Non-people sources of extrinsic FB

Feedback doesn't have to come from another person. There are other sources of feedback available to hitters if they just know where to look for it. The choice is up to you as to how much you want to use multiple sources of extrinsic FB. Other sources of extrinsic FB include but are not limited to:

- *Video feedback.* Many softball programs have access to a camcorder. If you have access, videotaping yourself is possibly the best thing you can do to improve your swing both physically and mentally. Videotaping your practice will allow you to see yourself in a low-competitive setting in which you are probably more relaxed and hitting better, and you can change the angles to view your swing from various perspectives. Recording during a game will allow you to examine your emotional control during your at-bats, your choice of pitches to swing at, and your overall physical performance in a high- competitive setting. If you are

Criminally insane batting coaches.

lucky and your coaches have access to programs that break down your swing frame by frame, use them. Not only might they find what is wrong with your swing, but they may also reveal what you are doing well and what you can do to make your next at-bat better.

- *Bat feedback*. Have you ever noticed that after you hit the ball, a residue from the ball is left on your bat? This is a great way to see exactly how much of the ball you made contact with and on which part of the bat. This will allow you to understand the reason your ball traveled the way it did during your at-bat. If you are going to use this kind of feedback, you must always clean your bat before every game. If you share a bat with a teammate, make sure to wipe off old scuff marks so you don't get confused as to which marks are yours.

- *Statistical feedback*. Looking at your statistics can provide numerical feedback that is very accurate. Just by looking at your strikeouts, batting average, doubles, home runs, etc., you can see what areas need work and where you can make a bigger impact. Do not depend solely on statistics, however, because they only tell part of the story of what really happens during your at-bat.

Sources of intrinsic feedback

Intrinsic FB is any information the hitter obtains from her five senses during a movement. Hitters primarily rely on three sources of intrinsic FB: visual, kinesthetic and auditory.

- *Visual feedback.* This type of FB provides any information the hitter obtains by watching what is happening. Visual FB is extremely important for a hitter's timing. The hitter picks up the rhythm of the pitcher's motion by watching her pitch. The type of pitch thrown is picked up by watching the pitcher's motion and by watching the path and flight of the ball. When watching a pitcher, see if you can identify differences in the timing or motion that can provide the hitter with information about the pitch. For example, many pitchers shorten their stride when pitching a drop (to get on top of the ball), lengthen their stride when pitching a rise ball (to get under the ball), extend their arm out straight when pitching a fast ball (to increase arm/lever length), or shorten their arm length when pitching a curve (to provide more spin). These changes in timing and/or motion can provide valuable information to the hitter.

- *Kinesthetic feedback.* This type of FB is derived from what it feels like when the swing is executed. It's referred to as the "feel" of the swing. When you take a swing that doesn't feel right, you know right away that your swing is off. You try to get the feeling back and when you do, everything seems to be fine again. Kinesthetic FB is used by hitters because after years and years of hitting, the hitter knows when she is not hitting well just by the feel of the swing. Take into account, though, that this taps into the "be comfortable with feeling uncomfortable" concept. Too many players focus so much of the time on feeling right that when they are not feeling right they fail miserably or panic during their at-bat. It's okay to want to feel good when you're swinging at practice or during a game, but it's not okay to have to feel right in order to do well. Hitters waste more at-bats trying to feel good rather focusing on the routine.

- *Sound feedback.* Sound or auditory FB is obtained by listening to the sounds around you. Hitters (as well as fielders) learn quickly what a solid hit sounds like when the bat contacts the ball. When the bat does not hit the ball squarely you can hear a sound that is not normal. When you get jammed or knick the edge of the ball with your bat you may hear a "thud" sound instead of the regular "ping" (if it's an aluminum bat) you're used to. This FB allows you to know exactly how your bat contacted the ball without seeing or feeling it. The sound of the hit can tell you when the ball is hit correctly and solidly or when you need to make adjustments. If you don't notice the sound when you are hitting, watch other players bat and listen to the sound of their ball hitting the bat when they hit well or poorly. You can hear a definite difference and understand whether they got jammed or barely hit the ball. Sometimes when you swing, you may not be able to feel or see what you did, but you can definitely hear.

- *Feedback sheets.* FB sheets can be valuable tools to help you understand more of the available FB around you. The purpose of these sheets is to encourage the hitter to think about and evaluate her hitting performances and the factors that might facilitate or hinder them. This information can be readily provided by yourself and your coaches. Pooling the FB from numerous sources can be very useful in identifying what might be happening when you step into the batter's box. When hitters are in stressful situations they can develop tunnel vision. Tunnel vision means focusing on too little information, thus missing out on important performance information. Feedback sheets can provide a better overall understanding of what you and others see as hitting strengths and weaknesses. This FB can then provide a direction for future improvement. Following are examples of self-evaluative and coach-evalu-

SELF-EVALUATION FEEDBACK SHEET

Game: Date:

1. List some stressors you had to deal with during the game in your at-bats:

2. How did you experience the stress?

3. What did you do to cope with the stress?

4. What could you have done better to cope with the stress?

5. How was your pre-performance routine for each at-bat?

6. How many of your at-bats were quality at-bats?

   Why were they quality at-bats?

7. How many of your at-bats did you give away?

   Why did you give them away?

8. What was one enjoyable thing about this game?

9. Based on your hitting performance in this game, what goals will you set for the next game?

COACH'S EVALUATION FEEDBACK SHEET

Hitter: Game: Date:

1. Was this hitter stressed in the batter's box today?

2. Which at-bats were stressful?

3. What did the hitter do to cope with the stress?

4. What could the hitter have done better to cope with the stress?

5. How was the hitter's pre-performance routine for each at-bat?

6. How many of the hitter's at-bats were quality at-bats?

   Why were these quality at-bats?

7. How many of the hitter's at-bats were given away (not quality at-bats)?

   Why did the hitter give them away?

8. What was one thing you saw the hitter do well in this game?

9. Based on this hitter's performance in this game, what goals would you suggest for the next game?

ative feedback sheets that can be used to gather FB information.

These feedback sheets focus mainly on stressors and self-evaluation. There are many other kinds of feedback sheets that are created by coaches and performance-enhancement specialists. Some can focus solely on routines, goal setting, achievements, emotions, or whatever the person handing them out wants to learn from the athlete. The one great thing about feedback sheets is that you can create your own emphasizing any specific situation or game.

Here are some guidelines you may want to follow when making and using your own feedback sheets. You do not have to do it this way; these are only suggestions:

- Have them completed for games or tournaments (evaluating yourself after you've competed will give you the truest and most realistic FB).
- Start with general questions and lead up to specific ones.
- Limit the sheet to no longer than two pages (you may not have the time nor desire to write lengthy answers).
- Fill out the FB sheet 24-48 hours after the game (this will give you time to let emotions settle and think about how you did).
- Fill out a sheet every once in awhile (don't do it every game, you may overload yourself with too much

analysis; you may want to do it when you are hitting really well or really poorly).

- During tournaments, have one feedback sheet for the whole tournament (this will allow you to evaluate your overall performance for the series, not just one at-bat).

- Have a mark on the sheet to represent a good performance and a bad performance so that when needed it will be easier for you to distinguish the good evaluations from the poor ones.

THINGS TO REMEMBER:

1) Accept other people's criticism in a positive manner and remember to consider the source. Just because someone gives you FB doesn't mean you must follow it!

2) Your coaches, teammates and family are great sources of extrinsic FB, so listen!

3) There are many types of FB including videotaping, kinesthetic, sound, visual, verbal, statistical and written. Use as many sources as possible to develop a realistic view of your hitting performance.

4) Feedback sheets can be a great tool for tracking how you felt and performed during competitions for future reference.

Chapter 10
Practical Drills for
Mental Skill
Rehearsal

Terminology

3-4 hole: The hole in the infield defensive scheme between the first and second base defensive positions.

5-6 hole: The hole in the infield defensive scheme between the third base and shortstop defensive positions.

4-6 hole: The hole in the infield defensive scheme between the second base and shortstop defensive positions (right over second base).

Hitting tee: The tee from which the hitter hits the ball.

Inside pitch tee placement: Placement of the hitting tee simulating an inside pitch.

Middle pitch tee placement: Placement of the hitting tee simulating a middle pitch.

Outside pitch tee placement: Placement of the hitting tee simulating an outside pitch.

QAB: "Quality at bat." Refers to an at-bat that may be recorded as an out in the scorebook but results in something positive within the game (i.e., bunt advancing the runner(s), sac fly advancing/scoring runner(s), suicide bunt scoring a run, etc.).

Soft toss: When another person tosses the ball toward the hitter so the hitter can practice various aspects of hitting. The tosser kneels on one knee along the first baseline (for a right-handed hitter) or along the third baseline (for a left-handed hitter). The tosser keeps the tossing arm elbow at a 90-degree angle and all movement comes from the shoulder. The fingers merely open and the ball leaves the hand with little to no spin.

Soft toss "down the middle": The soft tosser uses the hitter's belt buckle as the target for the toss.

Soft toss "inside pitch": The soft tosser uses the hitter's front hip (left hip for a right-handed hitter and right hip for a left-handed hitter) as the target for the toss.

Soft toss "outside pitch": The soft tosser uses the hitter's back hip (right hip for a right-handed hitter and left hip for a left-handed hitter) as the target for the toss.

Strike zone: The rule book interpretation of the strike area is from the hitter's knees to the lower chest across the width of home plate.

Umpire's strike zone: The umpire's perception of a hitter's strike zone which can vary from umpire to umpire.

Preparation to hit

Purpose: To review the relevant information to help ensure a quality at-bat.

Equipment: Copy of the Preparations to Hit Checklist (see the follwing page) and a writing implement.

Set-up: The checklist can be used during any situation hitting drill. Prior to hitting, have the hitter complete the checklist of the three phases of hitting. Each hitter begins in the "in-the-hole" position and completes the "in-the-hole" section of the checklist while in this position. After a sufficient amount of time (which varies with each at-bat), the hitter moves into the "on-deck" position and completes the "on-deck" section of the checklist. Again, after a sufficient amount of time, the hitter moves into the "at-bat" position and completes that section of the checklist after her at-bat. Any score less than 45 shows room for improvement.

Mental tips:

1. Hitters need to learn that hitting preparation begins in the "in-the-hole" position, not when they step into the batter's box.

2. Each athlete should learn the checklist so that it becomes second nature while progressing through the three phases of hitting.

Preparations to hit checklist

Game: At-bat number:

"In-the-hole" position

Good Poor N/A

1. All of my hitting gear (bat, batting gloves, helmet, etc.) is in one easy to access location.   3   2   1
2. Assessed the game situation while putting on my batting gloves and helmet.   3   2   1
3. Moved into the "in-the-hole" location.   3   2   1
4. Performed my pre-hitting performance routine (stretching, swinging the bat, etc.).   3   2   1
5. Watched the game to look for what might be asked of me once at-bat (hit away, bunt, slap bunt, hit and run, etc.).   3   2   1
6. Reviewed my hitting plan for this at-bat.   3   2   1

"On-deck" position

1. Continued to loosen up and relax.   3   2   1
2. Timed the pitches by swinging the bat with each pitch.   3   2   1
3. Reviewed my hitting plan for this at-bat.   3   2   1

"At-bat" position

1. Walked out to the batter's box with confidence.   3   2   1
2. Received the sign from the coach.   3   2   1
3. Continued to revise or confirm my hitting plan in my head.   3   2   1
4. Performed my "at-bat" routine between each pitch.   3   2   1
5. Stepped out of the box between each pitch.   3   2   1
6. Once set in the box focused only on the ball in the pitcher's hand.   3   2   1

Overall I would rate this at-bat as: good   poor

One thing I need to work on is_____.

Learning your strike zone

Variation showing path of ball from the pitcher

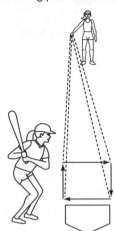

Purpose: While most rule books define the strike zone as the hitter's knees to the bottom of the chest (approximately the bottom of the letters on the uniform), perception of the strike zone varies from umpire to umpire. It is crucial for hitters to learn their strike zone and be able to widen or lengthen it as needed when playing with different umpires.

Equipment: Approximately 12' of string or rope.

Set-up: Have the hitter step into the batter's box and assume her batting stance. With the help of two people, the rope/string is held across the front of the plate at the bottom of the chest, down the inside of the plate to the knees, across the plate at knee level, and back up to the bottom of the chest along the outside of the plate, tjis creating a template of that hitter's strike zone (as shown on the previous page). Have the coach hold a ball in numerous locations along the outside of the strike zone, making sure that some portion of the ball is in the strike zone. Ask the hitter to create a template of the strike zone and commit it to memory. This needs to be done on numerous occasions for the hitter to accurately formulate the template.

Variations:

1. Have the hitter visualize themselves at bat (using internal imagery) while pitches are coming toward them. Have the hitter determine if the pitch is a ball or a strike by seeing the ball in relation to the template.

2. To help an athlete learn to pick up the ball as it is being pitched, use four additional 40' pieces of string/rope and a third person to be the pitcher. Have the two string/rope holders grasp one end of the 40' pieces of string/rope at each corner of the strike zone and the pitcher grasp the other ends out at the pitching mound. Have the pitcher hold all four pieces of string/rope in her right hand (to simulate a right-handed pitcher) or her left hand (to simulate a left-handed pitcher) to create a template showing the path of a pitch as it leaves the pitcher's hand to the strike zone.

Mental tips:

1. Make sure the hitters can create the strike zone template in an image. If they are having difficulty formulating or recalling the image, have them practice the basic imagery exercises described in this chapter.

Q charts for quality at-bats (QAB)

Purpose: To teach athletes that success in the batter's box 100 percent of the time is not only unlikely but IMPOSSIBLE!! Hitting in the game of softball is based on failure. If a hitter gets one hit every three at-bats that would be a .333 batting average which is pretty darn good! But that "pretty darn good" performance means that two of the three at-bats resulted in "not so goods." The idea behind QABs is to make sure that something positive comes from those two "not so good" at-bats. The positive elements are not apparent in the batting average or in most hitting statistics kept by the team to indicate at-bat performance. Hitters need to move beyond the typical hitting performance statistics and view each at-bat as an opportunity to make something positive happen for your team. Example of QABs:

Strike out:

Went after only good pitches.

Took good solid cuts rather than called strikes.

Made the pitcher pitch numerous pitches to get the out.

Fouled off numerous pitches in trying to stay the inning.

Sacrifice bunt:

Executed bunt to the correct location on the field.

Advanced the runner(s).

121

Forced the defense to make throws and to make the out.

Sacrifice fly:

Executed the sac fly to the correctlocation on the field.

Advanced the runner(s).

Forced the defense to make throws and make the out.

Solid hitting— ground ball:

Had a hitting plan.

Executed the hitting plan.

Hit the ball in the direction of the pitch (i.e., inside, outside and down the middle).

Waited for and recognized the pitch you were looking for.

Forced the defense to come up with a good defensive play.

Solid hitting— line drive:

Had a hitting plan.

Executed the hitting plan.

Hit the ball in the direction of the pitch (i.e., inside, outside and down the middle).

Waited for and recognized the pitch you were looking for.

Forced the defense to come up with a good defensive play.

Hitting execution:

Executed the hitting skill requested by the coach (i.e., bunt, slap, sac fly, etc.).

Ran on a dropped third strike by the catcher, safely reaching first base.

Ran on a dropped third strike by the catcher, advancing the runner(s).

Forced the defense to come up with a good defensive play.

Emotional control while at bat:

Was able to shake off the bad calls by the umpires.

Stayed with the hitting plan throughout the at-bat.

Revised the hitting plan when needed.

Demonstrated confidence during the at-bat.

Equipment: An assistant coach, team member, parent or volunteer to fill out Q charts for the entire game. Numerous pencils, an eraser, a clipboard and a stack of Q charts (one for each hitter).

Set-up: Have the Q chart keeper located in a place where he or she has a good view of the hitter, pitcher and strike zone. The Q chart keeper should be someone familiar and trustworthy enough to record game information.

Mental tips:

1. Following the game, a coach should review and evaluate the QABs for each hitter.

2. A coach should then meet with each hitter to review QABs and discuss any areas needing work, and any positive and negative tendencies from that game.

Q Chart

Name:_____#_____   Opponent:_____

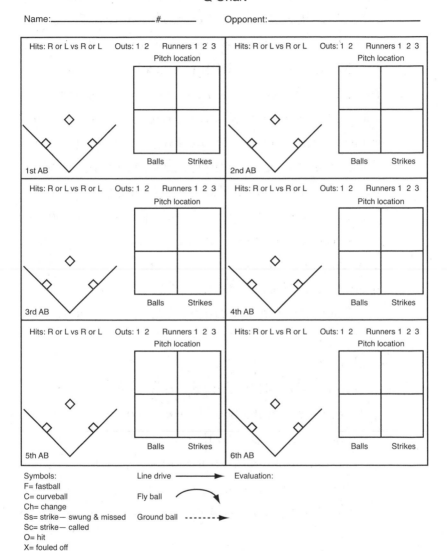

Hits: R or L vs R or L	**Outs:** 1 2	**Runners** 1 2 3

Pitch location

Balls   Strikes

1st AB

Hits: R or L vs R or L   Outs: 1 2   Runners 1 2 3
Pitch location
Balls   Strikes
2nd AB

Hits: R or L vs R or L   Outs: 1 2   Runners 1 2 3
Pitch location
Balls   Strikes
3rd AB

Hits: R or L vs R or L   Outs: 1 2   Runners 1 2 3
Pitch location
Balls   Strikes
4th AB

Hits: R or L vs R or L   Outs: 1 2   Runners 1 2 3
Pitch location
Balls   Strikes
5th AB

Hits: R or L vs R or L   Outs: 1 2   Runners 1 2 3
Pitch location
Balls   Strikes
6th AB

Symbols:
F= fastball
C= curveball
Ch= change
Ss= strike— swung & missed
Sc= strike— called
O= hit
X= fouled off

Line drive ———→
Fly ball
Ground ball -------→

Evaluation:

Creating a hitting plan

Purpose: To understand how to establish a plan and what the plan should take into account.

Set-up: Part of the hitting preparation should include the formulation of a hitting plan before ever stepping into the batter's box. This plan should be thought out, reviewed and/or revised during each phase of the preparation to hit ("in-the-hole," "on-deck" and "at-bat"). The hitter's plan must be flexible to accommodate the type of pitch thrown, the location of the pitch and the skill execution requested (i.e., hit away, hit and run, bunt, slap, etc.). Use the following checklist to ensure the development of an effective hitting plan. Any items circled "no" demonstrates room for improving the hitting plan.

Mental tips:

1. Hitters should be formulating a hitting plan before getting into the "in-the-hole" position, not when they step into the batter's box.

2. Each athlete needs to learn the three parts of the checklist so it becomes second nature while progressing through the three phases of hitting.

Hitting plan checklist

Game: At-bat number:

Situation

1.	Am I aware of the runners on base?	yes	no
2.	Am I aware of the defensive positioning?	yes	no
3.	Am I aware of how the pitcher is pitching?	yes	no
4.	Am I aware of the score?	yes	no
5.	Am I aware of the inning?	yes	no
6.	Do I need to widen or lengthen the strike zone for this umpire?	yes	no
7.	Does the coach's sign change my plan? If yes, then what is the new plan?	yes	no

Count

1.	What is the count the pitcher reaches?	yes	no
2.	What is my count?	yes	no
3.	Does this count require a change in my hitting plan?	yes	no
4.	If yes, do I know what change(s) I need to make to my plan?	yes	no

Pitch I am looking for

1.	Am I ahead or behind the count?	yes	no
2.	Do I know what pitch the pitcher goes to when ahead in the count?	yes	no
3.	Can I be choosy in selecting a pitch?	yes	no
4.	Do I know what pitch the pitcher goes to when behind in the count?	yes	no
5.	Do I need to alter the strike zone?	yes	no
6.	Do I need to protect the plate?	yes	no
7.	Does the coach's sign change the pitch I am looking for?	yes	no
8.	If yes, do I know what pitch am I looking for?	yes	no

Imagery exercises

Purpose: To help the hitter improve and understand how the mental skill of imagery can enhance hitting performance.

Equipment: Find a comfortable and quiet location to practice your imagery. Imagery scripts work best when a person reads the script aloud to you. You may also read the scripts into a recording device and then replay the tapes/CDs to practice your imagery on your own. These tapes/CDs are great to listen to before playing a game!

Mental tips:

1. Some individuals have good imagery skills and find the imagery exercises more distracting than helpful. If this describes you, then don't do these exercises.

2. Use imagery for those skills you can overtly (physically) execute. Imagery is not as effective for skills you are not able to perform.

Exercise #1: Vivid imagery

Close your eyes and imagine a softball. In your mind's eye slowly turn the ball and focus on any scuff marks or torn laces. Now see the ball lying on the green infield grass. Notice the contrast in the colors. Push the ball slowly across the grass and notice the seams rotate as the ball passes over the grass. See the ball roll to a stop and notice the location of the seams.

Exercise #2: Narrow focus < = > broad focus imagery

Close your eyes and imagine yourself standing at home on your softball field. In your mind's eye slowly turn your head as you survey the infield from third base to second base to first base. Focus on any marks, divots or holes on the field or on the bases. Now see how the infield dirt turns to green as you move your view toward the outfield. Notice the contrast in the colors. Survey left field, moving slowly into center field, then into right field. Focus on any marks, divots or holes on the field. Look at the outfield fence. Start in right field and slowly move your view to center field, on to left field, then back to center field. From center field slowly narrow your view from a wide angle to second base, to the pitching mound, and finally to home plate. Focus on home plate and notice the straight edges, the points and the colors.

Exercise #3: Internal imagery

Close your eyes and imagine yourself preparing to step into the batter's box from your own perspective. Slowly go through your performance routine. Don't limit the exercise by simply seeing yourself doing the routine but feel yourself also. Feel the bat in your hands, feel the deep breath, see the bat label, feel yourself step into the box and prepare the dirt in the box. Feel yourself set up for the pitch. Watch the pitcher pitch an inside fastball. Track the ball all the way to the catcher's glove and hear the ball hit the glove. See and feel yourself step out of the box, check your coach for signs, review your hitting plan and begin your performance routine again. Feel yourself going through your routine. Step back into the box and get set for the next pitch. Watch the pitcher pitch an outside fastball. Track the ball all the way to the catcher's glove and hear the ball hit the glove.

Exercise #4: External imagery

Close your eyes and see yourself preparing to step into the batter's box from an external perspective. See yourself slowly go through your performance routine. Notice how you hold the bat in your hands, and how you breathe. See yourself look at the bat label, step into the box and prepare the dirt in the box. See yourself set up for the pitch. Watch the pitcher pitch an inside fastball. Track the ball all the way to the catcher's glove and hear the ball hit the glove. See yourself step out of the box, check your coach for signs, review your hitting plan and begin the performance routine again. See yourself going through your routine. Notice how you step back into the box and get set for the next pitch. Watch the pitcher pitch an outside fastball. Track the ball all the way to the catcher's glove and hear the ball hit the glove.

Exercise #5: Past Successful Performance imagery

Close your eyes and recall a successful hitting experience from a past game. Using external imagery (visualizing yourself from the dugout), remember all you can about that experience prior to the performance. What color uniform were you wearing? What bat did you use? What number hitter were you that inning? How many outs were there? Where were the runners? See yourself in the "in-the-hole" position. What can you see yourself doing? Now see yourself in the "on-deck" position. What can you see yourself doing? See yourself step into the batter's box. What can you see yourself doing? See yourself execute that at-bat in slow motion. Did you see the ball come off the bat? See the ball travel through the air. See yourself leaving the batter's box with a smile on your face.

Now using internal imagery (visualizing yourself from within your own body), remember all you can about that same at-bat experience. What color uniform were you wearing? What bat did you use? How did the bat feel in your hands? What number hitter were you that inning? How many outs were there? Remember all you can about your "in-the-hole" experience. What were you thinking about? Remember all you can about your "on-deck" experience. What were you thinking about? Remember all you can about the at-bat. What were you thinking about by that phase? See yourself execute the at-bat in slow motion. How did you feel?

Exercise #6: Creating a successful image

Close your eyes and use internal imagery to picture yourself preparing to step into the batter's box after receiving the "hit away" sign from your coach. Do more than simply see yourself perform your pre hitting routine, feel yourself perform it also. See and feel yourself step into the box, prepare the dirt and settle your feet and get set for the pitch. Focus on the pitcher as she begins her windup so you can locate the ball as soon as possible. See the pitcher release the ball and watch the seams rotating as the ball travels toward you. See the ball traveling out of the strike zone and make the decision not to swing. Feel yourself hold up on the pitch. Hear the ball hit the catcher's glove and hear the umpire say "ball." See and feel yourself step out of the box, and look at the coach for a sign. There is no change in the sign so you begin your pre-hitting routine again. See and feel yourself step into the box, prepare the dirt and settle your feet and get set for the next pitch. Focus again on the pitcher in order to find the ball as soon as possible. See the pitcher release the ball and watch the seams rotating as the ball travels toward you. See the ball traveling right down the middle of the strike zone and make the decision to swing. See and feel yourself stride toward the ball, your hands pulling through and the bat head picking up speed. Hear the ball hit the bat. Feel the tightness in your body as the bat swings through the ball. See and feel yourself stride out of the box as you sprint toward first base and drop the bat. Sneak a peek at your hit then look at the first base coach to pick up the run signs. See the "round and hold" sign, feel yourself make your cut to hit the inside corner of the base, and then turn your head to locate the hit ball being fielded by the center fielder. See the center fielder field the ball cleanly and throw it to second base.

See and feel yourself put on the brakes, stop your forward progress, and return to first base where your first base coach is waiting to high five you!

Goal-setting exercise

Purpose: To help the hitter develop challenging but realistic short- and long-term goals.

Set-up: One way to introduce goal setting to hitters is to use the "staircase approach." Each hitter should identify her long-term goals for the season. Once the long-term goals are set, she must identify the short-term goals that will help her reach her long-term goals.

Mental tips:

1. Goals must be specific (identify exactly what is to be achieved), measurable (know when the goal is achieved) and observable (see the goal is met).
2. Set time limits for both short-term and long-term goals.
3. Set challenging but realistic goals.
4. Constantly evaluate and modify goals not being met.
5. Set process and performance goals not just outcome goals.
6. The achievement of the short-term goals should lead to the achievement of the long-term goal.
7. Set both team and individual goals.
8. Set goals in practices as well as in games.
9. Goals must be accepted by the individual athletes.

Goal-setting sheet

Use the following example to help set your short- and long-term goals for the season.

Long-term goal: <u>Hit .300 for the season</u>

	Practice daily	Practice weekly
Short-term goal:		
learn how to prepare to hit	x	
Short-term goal:		
develop my pre-performance routine	x	
Short-term goal:		
know my strike zone		x
Short-term goal:		
learn my hitting zone	x	
Short-term goal:		
widen and lengthen the strike zone		x
Short-term goal:		
fight off pitches		x
Short-term goal:		
create a hitting plan	x	
square around bunt	x	
pivot bunt	x	
slap bunt	x	
hit and run	x	
hitting to the left side	x	
hitting to the right side	x	
hitting up the middle	x	
Short-term goal:		
understanding QABs		x
strive for QABs (not just batting average)	x	

Hitting drill #1: Two tee focusing drill

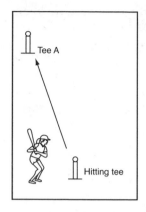 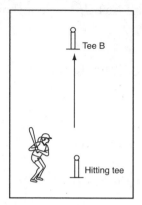 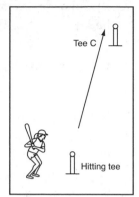

Purpose: To develop a feel for driving the ball toward a specific location on the field.

Equipment: Batting cage, four hitting tees and a bucket of tee balls.

Set-up: Place the hitting tee toward the back of the hitting cage. Place the second tee (Tee A) approximately 8'-10' to the left side (the 5-6 hole) of the batting cage, the third tee (Tee B) directly in front of the hitting tee, and the fourth tee (Tee C) to the right side (the 3-4 hole) of the batting cage. Tees A, B and C should have a ball on top. The hitter hits a sequence of nine balls off the hitting tee toward each tee (three balls per tee), with the goal being to knock the ball off the tees with each swing.

Variations:

1. Move the hitting tee to simulate inside and outside pitches and to demonstrate the difficulty in

136

trying to hit inside pitches toward the 3-4 hole and outside pitches toward the 5-6 hole.

2. Once hitters begin hitting the balls off Tees A, B and C, move the tees back 5'.

3. Once hitters begin hitting the balls off Tees A, B and C, raise and lower the hitting tee.

Mental tips:

1. Pretend the balls on Tees A, B and C are spots on the field that you want to hit it to.

2. Remember to drive the ball off the hitting tee with each swing.

3. Treat this drill as an at-bat. How many times will you fail before you are successful, and will frustration get the best of you if you cannot hit the ball off the tee frequently? Rehearse stepping out of the box, taking a deep breath (to relieve frustration) and stepping back into the box.

Hitting drill #2: Hula hoop focus drill

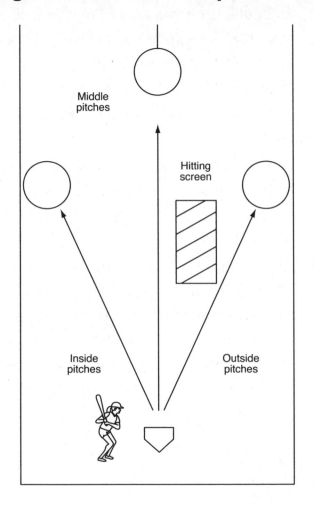

Purpose: To hit whatever pitch is pitched at you
through one of three hula hoops. For a right-handed
hitter, an inside pitch must be hit through the left
hoop, a pitch down the middle through the center
hoop, and an outside pitch through the right hoop.

Equipment: Three hula hoops, duct tape to fasten the hoops to the batting cage so that the center of the hoop is approximately 4-6' off the ground, a hitting tee and a bucket of tee balls.

Set-up: Tape the three hula hoops to the left, center and right sides of the batting cage (as shown on previous page), making sure the hoops are at line drive height. Have the hitter step into the batter's box following her routine. The hitter gets set as if waiting for the pitch, then hits the ball toward the appropriate hoop, depending on the setup of the hitting tee (i.e., the inside pitch toward the left hoop, the outside pitch toward the right hoop and the down-the-middle pitch toward the center hoop). Hit nine total balls (three toward each hoop) and then rotate.

Variations:

1. Have a coach or player pitch the ball from behind a hitting screen so the hitter learns to recognize inside, outside and down-the-middle pitches.

2. Once hitters begin hitting the balls through the hoops, raise and lower the hitting tee.

Mental tips:

1. The hoops represent the alleys where a hitter should strive to hit. Instead of just hitting anywhere in the cage, the hitter can use the hoops as a visual target for directing the ball and a way to determine her success in the cage.

Hitting drill #3: Gap focus drill

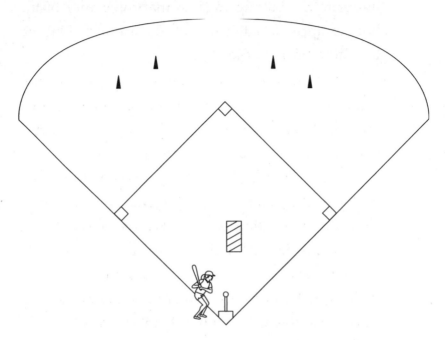

Purpose: To focus hitting the balls to specific locations on the field (between cones). This narrow focus helps hitters learn to drive the ball into the gaps on the field typically resulting in doubles and scoring runners when in scoring position (on second or third base).

Equipment: A hitting tee, a bucket of tee hitting balls and four cones.

Set-up: Place two cones in left center and two cones in right center (as shown above). Depending on the degree of difficulty the cones may be placed 5'-45' apart from each other. Have the hitter step into the batter's box following her routine. The hitter gets set as if waiting for the pitch, then hits the ball toward the appropriate gap, depending on the setup of the hitting tee (i.e., the inside pitch toward the left gap, the outside pitch toward the right gap and the down-the-middle pitch toward either the left or right gap). Hit nine total balls (three inside, three outside and three down-the-middle pitches) and rotate out.

Variations:

1. Once hitters begin hitting the gaps, raise and lower the hitting tee.

2. Have a player or coach pitch or throw front toss from the mound.

3. Increase the degree of difficulty by decreasing the size of the gaps.

Mental tips:

1. Assume there are outfielders outside of the cones and every ball hit outside the cones is considered an out.

2. Take time between pitches, pretend there is a runner on second every time with two outs. You must direct a hit between the cones to score the game-winning run.

Hitting drill #4: Two tee extension drill

Purpose: To work on staying through the ball longer on contact and to produce more power for a harder hit ball.

Equipment: Two hitting tees and a bucket of tee hitting balls.

Set-up: Start by placing the two tees 4"-6" apart with a ball on each tee (as shown on the following page). On the first try position both tees as if you are hitting it back up the middle. After every successful cut contacting both balls, place the second tee farther away from the first. See how far apart the tees can be placed with the hitter still hitting both balls off the tees. Repeat the drill with the inside pitch followed by the outside pitch.

Mental tips: Imagine this drill as an extension of your hit. The second ball is the path your hit will take if you stay through the ball longer on contact.

Inside pitch	Middle pitch	Outside pitch

Hitting drill #5: Hitting the little things drill

Purpose: To have quick hands using a thin, light bat and to work on keeping your eye on the ball. Since the objects used in this drill are so small you will have to really keep your head still and your eyes on the object all the way through contact. If you would like, make it a competition to see how many objects you can hit out of 20, for example.

Equipment: One thin lightweight wooden or metal bat, a regular hitting bat, a bucket of popcorn kernels, a bucket of golf ball-sized whiffle balls, a bucket of baseballs and a bucket of softballs.

Set-up: Have a person soft toss the popcorn kernels, followed by the whiffle balls, the baseballs and finally the softballs. For the popcorn kernels and whiffle balls use the lightweight bat; for the baseballs and softballs use the regular bat. The object of this drill is to swing the bat with a solid hit on each object. It may seem difficult at first because it takes a lot of focus to keep your eye on the smaller objects.

Variations:

1. Reverse the order of objects tossed (i.e., begin with the softballs, followed by the baseballs, the whiffle balls and the popcorn kernels). Remember to use the regular bat for the softballs and

baseballs and the light-weight bat for the whiffle balls and popcorn kernels.

Mental tips:

1. If you find it hard to hit the kernels, remember not to get frustrated. Use your routine if you need to get refocused. It is possible, with a little patience and extra focus, to hit the kernels and become very good at it.

2. This drill tries to simulate what the ball may look like when you are in a game and having a hard time seeing and hitting the ball. Many players who have this problem will say that they cannot see the ball, that it seems so small, or that they have a hard time picking it up. Pretend this drill is one of those instances. Strive to work on making contact. If you find yourself in this situation during a game, remember you have already prepared for it and can succeed with a little extra focus!

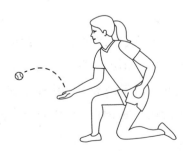

Hitting drill #6: Hitting for points drill

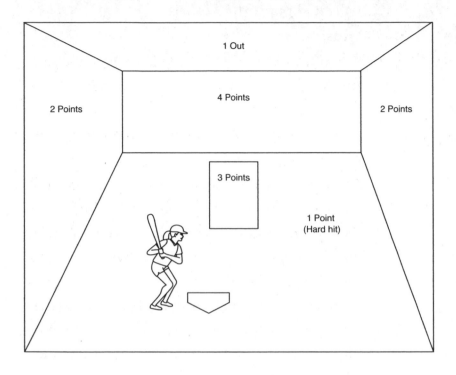

Purpose: To focus on hitting hard line drives while competing under pressure.

Equipment: A hitting tee and a bucket of tee hitting balls.

Set-up: In a batting cage have the hitter hit off the tee for points. Every hit is awarded the following points: A hard ground ball earns one point, a hard line drive to the side nets earns two points, a hard line drive back at the front toss net earns three points, and a hard line drive at the back of the net earns four points. A pop-up, soft ground ball or soft line drive is an out. Each hitter gets three outs per round. Go for as many rounds as you like while competing with a teammate or teammates.

Variations:

1. Raise and lower the hitting tee.
2. Move the hitting tee to simulate inside, outside and down-the-middle pitches.
3. Have someone front toss or pitch live while hitting.

Mental tips: During live pitching —

1. Pick your pitch to hit. Treat each round like an at-bat, lay off the balls and hit only the strikes. If you swing at bad pitches you will find that it will be hard to earn points.
2. Have the pitcher mix in a lot of change-ups if the drill seems to get easy for you. This will heighten the level of difficulty and help you practice hitting change-ups.

Bunting drill #1: Bucket bunting drill

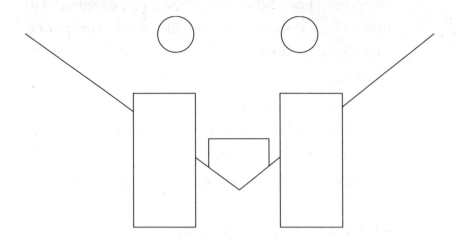

Purpose: To bunt the balls into the bucket by not bunting them too hard or too soft. The hitter must practice keeping the ball away from the catcher, pitcher, and first and third baseman. Bunting the ball toward a specific spot will give you the best chance to place the ball down and hopefully be safe.

Equipment: Two buckets and a bucket of hitting balls.

Set-up: In a batting cage or on the field place one bucket between the third-base position and the pitcher's mound. Place the second bucket between the first-base position and the pitcher. The buckets should be approximately 2'-3' in front of the batter's box. Have a player or coach pitch balls, or use a pitching machine. The hitter looks at the coach for the signal (typically in the first- or third-base coaching box). The coach signals either a first or third base bunt.

Following the bunt sign, the hitter steps into the box using her hitting routine and bunts the pitch to the requested location. See how many balls can be bunted into the buckets.

Variations:

1. Have the coach alternate between signals for either a slap bunt or a bucket bunt. Remind the hitter to slap bunt in the direction of the pitch (i.e., the inside pitch toward the 5-6 hole, the outside pitch toward the 3-4 hole, and the down-the-middle pitch toward the 4-6 hole).

Mental tips:

1. Before each bunt rehearse the signal that you will receive from your coach to bunt, bunt and run or squeeze. Know what you need to do in the situation before you get into the box. Focus on the two buckets to help you execute the bunt.

2. Pretend that for every executed bunt in the bucket your runner moves up one base. Try and score as many runners as possible with no runners on. For every missed ball in the bucket you get an out. For example, if you get the first ball in the bucket you get a runner on first. If you miss your second ball, you have one out with a runner on first. This is a great challenge, especially if you have another player to play against.

Bunting drill #2: Zone bunting drill

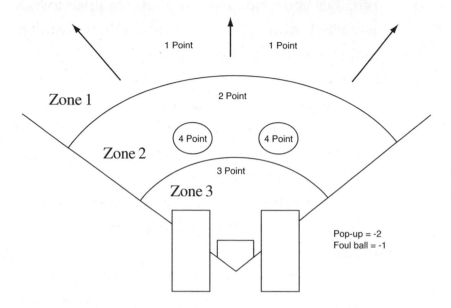

Purpose: To add competition pressure while focusing on getting the bunt down.

Equipment: Chalk and a bucket of hitting balls.

Set-up: Use white powder/chalk to mark off three zones in front of the batter's box (as shown above). Within the three zones mark a bonus zone in the alleys between third and pitcher, and first and pitcher. Give each zone a point value like Zone 1 = 1 point, Zone 2 = 2 points, Zone 3 = 3 points, and Bonus Zone = 4 points. For every foul ball subtract one point, and for every popped up ball subtract two points. Use either a live pitcher or a pitching machine, keeping track of each hitter's point totals to monitor bunting success.

Mental tips:

1. Focus on what needs to be done and where you can get the most points. Sometimes just getting the bunt down is all that's needed to win the game.

2. If you find yourself afraid of popping up or fouling the ball off, remember to use your routine and to keep it simple. Your job is to get the ball on the groundand move the runner over. If you are safe at first that is a bonus!

Slap bunting drill #1: Gap slapping focus drill

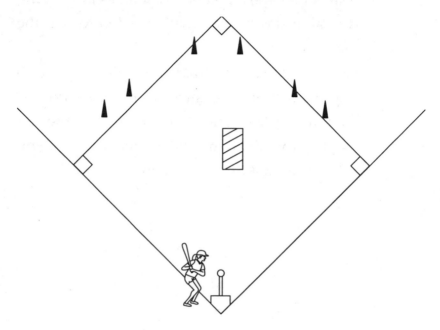

Purpose: To focus slapping the ball to specific locations on the field (between cones). This narrow focus helps hitters learn to slap the ball into the fielding gaps, typically resulting in advancing the runners or scoring runners when in scoring position (third base).

Equipment: A hitting tee, a bucket of tee hitting balls and six cones.

Set-up: Place two cones in the 5-6 hole gap, two cones in the 4-6 hole gap, and two cones in the 3-4 (as shown above). Depending on the degree of difficulty, the cones may be placed 3'-6' apart from each other. Have the hitter step into the batter's box following her routine. The hitter gets set as if waiting for the pitch, squares around to bunt, then slaps the ball toward the appropriate gap depending on the location of the pitch (i.e., the inside pitch toward the 5-6 hole gap, the outside pitch toward the 3-4 hole gap and the down-the-middle pitch toward the 4-6 hole gap). Slap nine total balls (three inside pitches, three outside pitches and three down-the-middle pitches) and rotate out.

Variations:

1. Once hitters begin hitting the gaps, raise and lower the hitting tee.

2. Have a player or coach pitch or throw front toss from the mound.

3. Increase the degree of difficulty by decreasing the size of the gaps.

Mental tips:

1. Assume that there are infielders positioned outside the cones and every ball hit outside the cones is considered an out.

2. Take time between pitches, pretend there is a runner on second every time with two outs. You must get a hit in between the cones to score the game-winning run.

References

Cluck, B. (2002). *Think Better Baseball*. New York, NY: Contemporary Books.

Cumming, J. L., & St. Marie, D. (2001). The cognitive and motivational effects of imagery training: a matter of perspective. *The Sport Psychologist*, *15*, 276-288.

Gould, D., Hodge, K., Peterson, K., & Giannini, J. (1989). An exploratory examination of strategies used by elite athletes' coaches to enhance self-efficacy in athletes. *Journal of Sport & Exercise Psychology*, *11*, 128-140.

Hackfort, D., & Schwenkmezger, P. (1993). Anxiety. In R. N. Singer, M. Murphy, & L. K. Tennant (Eds.), *Handbook of Sport Psychology* (pp. 328-364). New York: Macmillan.

Joseph, J. (2002). *The Softball Coaching Bible*. Champaign, IL: Human Kinetics.

Ravizza, K., & Hanson, T., (1995). *Heads-Up Baseball: Playing the Game One Pitch at a Time.* Indianapolis, IN: Masters Press.

Suinn, R. (1980). Psychology and sports performance: principles and applications. In R. Suinn (Ed.), *Psychology in Sports: Methods and Applications* (pp. 26-36). New York: Macmillan.

Vealey, R. S. (1986). Imagery training for performance enhancement. *Applied Sport Psychology.* Palo Alto, CA: Mayfield Press.

Weinberg, R. S., & Gould, D. (1999). *Foundations of Sport and Exercise Psychology.* Champaign, IL: Human Kinetics.